A Girl
Behind
Dark
Glasses

JESSICA TAYLOR-BEARMAN

Hashtag PRESS

Published in Great Britain by Hashtag Press 2018

Text © Jessica Taylor-Bearman 2018
Cover Illustration © Ffion Jones 2018
Cover Design © Helen Braid 2018

A CIP catalogue for this book is available from the British Library.

ISBN 978-1-9998053-5-7

Typeset in Garamond Classic 11.25/14 by Blaze Typesetting

Printed in Great Britain by Clays Ltd, Elcograf S.p.A

Hashtag PRESS

HASHTAG PRESS BOOKS
Hashtag Press Ltd
Kent, England, United Kingdom
Email: info@hashtagpress.co.uk
Website: www.hashtagpress.co.uk
Twitter: @hashtag_press

One Stupid Dot

Me and M.E Same letters separated by a dot
One's who I am, one's what I've got
One's who I used to be, one's what I'm not
Oh I'm still me, there's just a dot in-between
But it's a dot that can stop you from living a dream
It's a dot that separates the M from the E
And while it's sat there it's hard to be me
The 'me' that I was in healthier days
Before the dot came forcing the parting of the ways
I'm nothing as M and empty as E
But side by side again I could be me
That dot has got a lot to explain
How can something so small cause so much pain?
So much devastation, Seems endlessly cruel
It's just one stupid dot after all
Why does it have to be stuck in the middle?
Causing complex symptoms that read like a riddle?
I have to believe that just as it came
The dot will mysteriously vanish again
Every night before sleeping I hope and I pray
That I'll wake up as me without a dot in the way

By Mama Chill
© Mama Chill
www.officalrunningonempty.com

May my Eagle fly high on the wings of freedom.

Acknowledgements

With Special Thanks to Elizabeth Ann Giles, for inspiring me throughout her life. Chuckles and Mumsie. Tom and Becky. Pop. Nick. To my Grampy and Grandma. And most importantly, to my better half, Samuel.

This book would not have been possible without the Kickstarter supporters; especially Ruth Ann Harnisch and Amy Gilbert.

Preface

My name is Jessica. I am severely unwell and I tell you this story not for recognition, nor for my own pleasure, but to tell a story that needs to be told. This book was made possible only through a diary called Bug that I first started before I became unwell and continued through my illness. I suffer with a disease that you probably know little about. Some will have never heard of it, whilst fellow sufferers will know it all too well.

I have severe Myalgic Encephalomyelitis, commonly shortened to M.E., as it is not the easiest of medical jargons to pronounce. It is a deeply debilitating, chronic disease that you may know of as chronic fatigue syndrome (CFS). To me, the latter name is daft as it sounds like 'very tired syndrome' and that doesn't begin to describe the suffering, not in the slightest! I had never even heard of the condition until 2006 and had absolutely no idea of the symptoms or what it meant. That was the year my life changed forever.

The medical world knows little about M.E., its causes or why some people suffer more severely than others. It is a neurological condition that cunningly creeps up on you without anyone else being particularly aware. It all seemed to happen in a bizarre mixture of speed and slow motion. When I was fourteen, just before my fifteenth birthday to be precise, I became unwell with a flu-like virus and that was where my journey began.

I was living in the protective bubble of childhood. I didn't want to be ill. Who does? I took the typical British approach. After the initial virus was gone, I turned a blind eye to what was left behind. The demands of my day-to-day life started to come with a cost; multiple infections and viruses followed. Even then, I tried to carry on. I just wanted to be a kid. At the time, my philosophy was simple—I don't want to be ill, so I won't be.

Unfortunately, it was completely the wrong approach. Before long, I became housebound, as the M.E. Monster waged war with my body, torturing every cell, charging through my veins. I can still remember the day when I finally asked for help from the medical profession—help that they lacked the knowledge or understanding to give.

CHAPTER ONE

Before the Dot

I always thought of my family as being average. My parents weren't well off, but they weren't so totally strapped for cash that they couldn't give me, my brother, and my sister opportunities either, and that's all that mattered to them. Mum and Dad worked their socks off; my mum as a nurse practitioner and my dad as a paramedic, with the accompanying shift patterns.

Being from a medically-trained family, there was no expectation of having Christmas or birthdays off work. In fact, more often than not, Christmas was just another working day for my parents. The intense schedules never caused me or my siblings to be unhappy, instead it created an unbreakable bond between us all.

Dad worked eight Christmases in a row. Even though it was hard for a young family to understand why Dad wouldn't be around on Christmas Day, we spent magical holidays at my Gran and Pop's (my mum's parents).

I remember one Christmas Eve that I spent with Mum and Dad, so it was particularly special. It was from the days of being too young to know that the red lights in the sky came from planes, and I could have sworn I was seeing Father Christmas in his sleigh. This was confirmed by my parents and I had to continue being a 'good girl' to make sure Santa found my stocking that Christmas Eve as we drove to see my grandparents.

My brother Tom and I are best friends. It has always been like that. Before Becky was born, we lived in a small townhouse, where we shared a room. Tom was five years older than me and had a reserved character, dark blond hair, a tall frame and a very chilled-out manner. He was my hero.

We complemented each other perfectly: he was relaxed, I was on the go all the time—I wanted to walk even before I learned to speak. Tom was easy; as long as he could sleep and eat, he was fine. In contrast, I was awake all the time.

Our only similarity was that we were both content. Everything that Tom could do, I wanted to do. As soon as I could talk, I named the beloved bear I took everywhere, 'Tom Ted.' I would rather play with Tom and Tom Ted than with other little ones my own age.

When my parents were asked to use five words to describe me, Dad answered with a wry smile: happy, energetic, thoughtful, intelligent and mischievous. I'd had an infectious zest for life since birth. His Jessica Laura Elizabeth Taylor.

When I was four, I found out that I was going to be a big sister and I couldn't have been more excited. I didn't know why I was becoming a big sister, but I could see the bump in Mummy's tummy. Every night before bed, I talked to her stomach and told the bump that I loved it and that I hoped I would be able to play with baby as much as I did with Tom.

After what seemed like an eternity, my sister was born. In fact, I remember that I was with my Grandma and Grampy waiting for her to be born. We waited all day, until finally after the eighth phone call of the evening, she was born on the 21st May 1995. I had wanted to name her Lucy after my favourite doll I had lost outside, as a result of trying to make her friends with the wild guinea pigs. This request was only partially successful, and my little sister was registered as Rebecca Lucy Isobel Taylor.

She cried a lot. In fact, that's an understatement. She cried almost all the time, screwing up her bright blue eyes as she wailed.

"She's not like Lucy, Mummy!" I said with a sad face.

I started to share a small box room with her—it seemed a good idea at the time, although she cried all night!

Whilst our parents worked so hard to keep us afloat, both my grandparents played a huge part in our lives. We spent the majority of our time with Gran and Pop looking after us. This was never a chore. She always had a twinkle in her eye and bought us little treats, most often a chocolate bar.

They would take hold of my hands and say the words, "boing boing." It was my cue to try and jump as far as I could. Somehow, it felt like I could fly with those words. From my perspective, I really did soar a few steps further along the pavement.

They lived in a massive Victorian house with a brilliant garden full of greenery to explore. We played make-believe games with my cousins.

In the middle of the night we had a magical time visiting Fairyland, by day we went to Dolphin Land and Frog Land. We ran and played together, involving Becky and my youngest cousin too.

Our cousins lived just a village away from Gran and Pop,

so it was easy to go around to their house where there was a six-foot trampoline. One Boxing Day was spent bouncing, laughing and enjoying life. That is what being a child should be all about, and for me, it was.

*

We spent time with my dad's parents, Grandma and Grampy, too. There we would do a lot of gardening and growing vegetables. One of their traditions was to read the newspaper in the morning. Both Becky and I were staying over, and to keep us from disturbing them, my Grandma bought us each a magazine for every day we were with them. It certainly kept us busy and quiet too!

We alternated between our grandparents' homes throughout the school holidays. Whilst Gran kept my imagination running wild through teaching me to creatively write—we were going to write a book together you see—Pop taught me to sing. Grampy and Grandma kept me busy with learning to grow plants and how to knit. This carried on for many happy years.

When I was ten, our childminder came to pick us up early. We were jumping about excited to be leaving school half an hour early, our childminder looked troubled. It didn't really occur to me to wonder what was on her mind.

Once we got home, she sat us down and then she broke the news I was least expecting: my grandma had gone to sleep and never woken up. I wasn't going to see Grandma again. It had only been a few weeks prior that we had spent time together. I wasn't given a reason for my loss. A single tear fell down my face. Becky and Tom didn't speak. I just wanted to be hugged by all those I loved.

*

I was about to sit the Eleven Plus (an exam set in parts of England to determine what type of secondary school you would go to) but I was numb.

"She's gone to a better place," the adults kept saying.

It didn't make it better. Not in the slightest. Maybe it made them feel better? When I was picked up that evening, I hugged every member of Team Taylor.

"At least I can say sugar now," said Becky with satisfaction.

We all laughed. Grandma had been funny when we went for a caravan trip with them. We kept getting told off every time any of us said 'sugar' because she assumed we must have been using it to replace some naughty expletive. Genuinely, we were simply saying 'sugar' because we meant nothing more sinister than 'sugar'!

To deal with the loss, my Gran taught me to keep a diary. I had called my diary Bug and had started with trying to write about how I was feeling on a special notepad she gave me.

All of us had to take a day off school to attend the funeral. I had never been to a funeral before and wasn't sure what to wear or even what it would be like.

On Dad's request I wore a kilt and white shirt. Pop played the organ and Gran held my hand. Tom held my other hand, and for the first time in my life, my brother sobbed. I gave his hand a squeeze. It was the first and last time that I saw my brother cry. I began to cry too.

Towards the end of the service, Grampy got up to try and help carry the coffin with Dad and his brothers. He let out the most horrendous mourning noise, almost like a cry for help. It sounded so painful, and again, that was the first and last time I heard Grampy cry. It was a terrible sight to behold.

I vowed to write to my diary, Bug, that evening to tell him how horrible it had all been. To ask him why it had happened. Little did I know, the next few years of diary writing would be pivotal in documenting my own health decline.

CHAPTER TWO

Extracts from a Diary Called Bug
September 2005 – November 2006

September 10th 2005
Dear Bug,

Telling the epic adventure of Jess Taylor from the beginning would be a rather long story, I imagine. I am always practising writing and have been fascinated by the idea of keeping a diary but could never keep it going before; my life has always been too busy to put pen to paper. Awesome news! The book that Gran and I have been planning, since that holiday to France, is in full flow. We are making characters up as we speak. Maybe our first book could be about the journeys of Jess and Gran? We always liked this idea but if we were going to get anywhere, I will have to think seriously about you, Bug!

I have passed my design and technology GCSE two years early with flying colours and am living life to the full. Being a fourteen-year-old means: late(r) nights, partying hard, family time and working hard too!

I will be honest. I'm not a fan of the name Jessica, it sounds too formal when people call me that. I've felt like that about it forever, especially since starting secondary school. Its formal sound just reminds me of rules. I'm not one to follow rules, in fact, I'm a rule bender! You must live in the moment, enjoying every second. As my parents always remind us when Becky and I are playing up:

"There are people in Africa in poverty far worse off than you, so pack it in!"

We generally do 'pack it in' but not without me pointing out that, if I just had my own room, things would be different.

We went to Scotland for our summer holiday this year. I remember feeling the sea breeze tickle my hair as I watched with great intent to catch sight of the dolphins of the Moray Firth, the picturesque scenery filling my mind's eye. Oh, and the quad biking with my dad! That was heavenly freedom, zooming across the Scottish valley with not a worry on my mind. I will definitely be doing that next year. Best of all, I spent it with the people that I love most dearly, whom it was fun to just lark around with. I was just me, the crazy young lady who is full of ideas and has places to be. I have so much to tell the world! It seems ludicrous to me that there are people who enjoy doing nothing with their lives, that's just not me.

I will let you into a secret, if you promise not to say anything? I love going to school. I love learning and back-chatting the teachers (never rudely, of course). I am all about charm and wit mixed with a good measure of humour too! Meeting and being with different people and using a completely different part of my personality. Naughty but nice in equal measures. Got to go now, the phone has rung—it's just past 6pm so the calls are free! And I've got as many conversations going on MSN as I have fingers.

"Jess, you said you were doing homework but all I can see

is a hundred and one conversations." Bummer. . . caught in the act as well.

"I am doing work of some sorts, look!"

I'm using you, Bug, as evidence of my work; it's not lying, just 'stretching the truth' somewhat. I am deep in thought . . .

"Jess, off that computer now!"

Mums really do have the final say.

Love always,

Jess

October 13th 2005

Dear Bug,

Oops, I think things got a little bit rowdy today at school (I'm trying to develop my vocabulary). It was hilarious and a bit of mayhem too! My friend brought in some vodka and managed to successfully get it through the gates in a water bottle.

"Geez, do you know how much trouble we'd be in if we were caught?" I said, rather flippantly.

"Yeah, but the point is we won't get caught, will we?! Just down a bit of it and we'll have a good day," said one friend.

I knew she meant business so, to not look like a wuss, I drank it and more than my fair share so the other girls wouldn't get in trouble. We are known as rule benders but I just hoped to hell that I had the strong Taylor gene for being able to handle drink. Turns out I do, so all was well.

It was funny. We're all young, free, imaginative kids, wanting to live our freedom. Not really hard nuts trying to hurt others. That makes it okay for now but I know I won't EVER be telling Mum and Dad this! LOL! (Laugh out loud—in case I ever let somebody else read this who does not know.) We're now legends at school, really tough to have even thought of doing it. I'm rolling my eyes just thinking about it.

I'm told that I'm using my grammar incorrectly at school, so I will be trying to go back and correct myself. It is important to me to do well. I believe wholeheartedly that if you aren't going to put all your effort in to something then there is no point in doing it at all. Life is made up of so many different moments, almost as many as there are stars in the sky. You have to pluck at them as they go past and live for every moment that you grab. That's one really philosophical thought, eh?

Love always,

Jess

29th December 2005

Dear Bug,

Christmas was spectacular this year for a very different reason. I managed to do the most random thing ever. On Christmas Day, it's essential to have the Taylor tradition of crumpets with a layer of butter on top for breakfast. There is nothing more scrummy than this. As I went to do this family tradition, I managed to get the crumpet stuck in the toaster. I went to move it slightly with that moment of ludicrously thinking I could move the crumpet from the toaster without scalding my hand.

Alas, it did not work and instead, as my finger touched the hot toaster, with reflexes that had pinpoint accuracy, my wrist bone flung into the corner of the cupboard quicker than I could think. The pain came pulsing into my hand and that was it. I had broken my wrist. No matter how many bags of frozen peas I used! We then had to improvise and it soon became frozen sweetcorn because we were quickly defrosting the peas.

Tom drove me to meet Dad (who had been at work) at A&E, and my arm was put into a sling, which I wasn't allowed to move. Devastatingly, that is six weeks off netball. I didn't even get to eat the sodding crumpet. However, it didn't stop there.

Once the school term had begun, everyone but everyone was getting sick. I was no different and before I knew it the whole class was off with this weird virus including me. This is where I am writing you from Bug, if I stand up or move my head to quickly, then I go dizzy and collapse. This is not such a clever thing when you are also one arm down so I am sitting in bed. I'm hoping it doesn't last too long—I've got exams to prepare for. Plus, I have got my birthday coming up. I will be fifteen and I can't wait. It is so boring being sick.

Love Jess

January 5th 2006
Dear Bug,

I have my first real boyfriend, as of today. I'm not talking about the one I had when I was four. Cringe! Before becoming my boyfriend, *Mark was a really good friend, alongside my friend Nick. We had been at church together but Mark was the only straight guy out of the pair so naturally. . . hormones go on overload and this is the result, but I am happy.

(*Mark was a year older than me, and although he made me happy, I was a very awkward teenager when it came to boys. He was a tad on the lanky side, incredibly skinny with dark eyes and rather a lot of pimples but at that time he made me happy. That was all that mattered.)

Mark walked me up the road to school, holding my hand, then we stopped. I nervously stood there thinking about what was about to happen and soon, before I knew what had happened, we were kissing.

So, that's what all the fuss is about, Bug! My first kiss and I'm not going to lie by telling you how romantic it was, because it's not like what we grow up believing—that it will be like a fairy tale.

It made me feel good though, so I must have done something right. I walked into school with a big grin on my face. I wonder if I was any good?

Love always,

Jess

February 20th 2006

Dear Bug,

If only you could have the fortune of meeting Nick. He's my bestie, through and through. We have known each other since we were little. The only thing that is annoying about him is, not only is he genuinely right about everything, but my 'babes' (that's was what we call each other) is stupidly talented. He can speak both French and German so, to help me out with a French oral examination, he wrote my spiel. Big mistake! Yes, it looked perfect, but I had no idea what he had written. It's anything for an easier life these days though, as my body is aching profusely.

Anyway, it got to the examination and the teacher was looking at me with a horrified expression when I spoke. I then decided to go on Google Translate and typed in what he had written for me.

My face dropped. What a little bastard! Argh! I'm going to

kill him! He had written that 'my dad had alcoholic tendencies,' that 'my mum didn't feed us' and 'my brother used to get girls off the street and wasn't clear on his sexuality.' CRINGE!

He took one look at me as he saw me walking out of school and burst into laughter, before fleeing to the bus stop.

"You should have done your own homework!" he said, still laughing.

Love always,

Jess

28th February 2006

Dear Bug

Alright love? How's it going? I think of you as a real person, someone in the future reading about my life.

I went to my grandparents' house today. You may think of it as an arduous task but it is quite the opposite for me. My gran is just the epitome of 'cool' and then times that by a hundred! I spent hours shopping in the city with her, then we had lunch at one of the many cafés. Naughty but nice in equal measures! Going home, it was a particularly cold day; my fingers were numb because I had been holding too many bags. We arrived at my grandparents' home to see the chimney billowing, advertising the joy of a toasty open fire in the lounge, managed by my Pop. Bliss!

Things aren't the same anymore though, it is tiring to do anything and I feel too tired to really think of anything else. Before, every time I went to my grandparents' I would sing with Pop. He is a brilliant pianist and singer, so I would sing and enter the world of music, flying free. Yet today, my voice was patchy and out of tune.

"Are you sure you are well? You are looking quite pale, chick." Pop said, as Gran hugged me.

"Just an off day, I think," I mumbled even though I knew my mask was starting to fall.

Love always,

Jess

1st March 2006

Dear Bug,

I've got to admit something to you, Bug. I've not been too well. Ever since that flu bug hit me, I just haven't felt like I fully got my mojo back. I'm exhausted and there is this pain in my legs like I've never experienced before. It's annoying because I am finding excuses to not go trampolining. Maybe it's just growing pains? I'm sure that is what the doctor would say and who would look like a prat then?

It's a weird old feeling, like reaching for something that is just out of reach. Car journeys are strange. They can be two minutes long or an hour long, but I have to sleep. The noise. I mean have you ever listened to how loud a car sounds? Was meant to be at an all-nighter party last night. Firstly, I have more sense than to even attempt that, but secondly, I couldn't have managed it; I need to rest.

There is a dull thud in my head, constantly, like a pulse thudding away in the quiet. No one notices it but how could they? Extra stress that no one needs. You see I am very good at hiding it. I'm British, that is what we Brits do, well, the ones I know. We suffer silently and fight on. One would have to be at death's door to actually go see someone about it. The thudding will stop. Thud. Thud. Thud. It will stop. Anyway, it's not going to beat me, or worry me, whatever it is, I will fight it, I've just got to put it to the back of my mind and that way it will go away. I've got another party to go to anyway, so no time to be ill! Thud. Thud. Thud. It will stop.

Love always,

Jess

26th March 2006

Dear Bug,

We went to see the Lion King at the theatre in London for my fifteenth birthday! It was my surprise present. I'm trying to take my mind off the exhaustion I am enduring with every breath. Sometimes I can think for a moment that everything is back to normal, then it comes and bites me hard. Anyway, Mark came too and we were probably the cheesiest couple—the ones making out a lot of the time, in places that were probably not the most apt, like when we were at the Science Museum (!)

The theatre was mesmerising but the day after. . . are you kidding me?! I was flat out as if I was drunk on exhaustion. Mum put it down to being a 'normal teenager' and allowed me to sleep in. The problem was I hadn't been able to GET to sleep. I've never had this problem before. Thud. Thud. Thud. It's back again but, in truth, it never properly left.

Love always,

Jess

8th May 2006

Dear Bug,

It's getting serious now. I forced myself to see the doctor. I haven't seen a doctor since I was a baby. They've told me I have a condition called 'post viral chronic fatigue syndrome,' which is also known as 'myalgic encephalomyelitis.' They gave me no 'get better' pill, no advice, but to rest.

Goddammit, I don't want to just rest! It's eating me up. I'm burning hot then I'm cold. I am exhausted but it's not like a tiredness I can explain. Let me tell you how today went:

I forced my eyes open, I heaved my body up, willing it to move with all my might. Determined to fight it, I staggered to the car: I slept in the car for the fifteen-minute drive. I got to school, yanking my body along, but I could barely make it up the stairs. I pretended to drop something as my legs fumbled. I held my head, my eyes throbbing. Small smiles and light conversation followed, then sleep. First lesson. Sleep. Second lesson. Rested my burning head. I was battling it like a warrior.

"Jessica! Get your head off the table!" the teacher shouted. Then my parents were called in. The amount of times I had told them I was okay because no frigging doctor was going to tell me what to do!

When I got home, I fell onto the sofa, barely able to move. My worried parents put a quilt over me and I just continued to rest. Little Becky came home from school on the very first day I had come home from school earlier than her. She looked at my pale, broken body and, instead of launching into one of the cat-and-dog fights we've always had since sharing a room, she just hugged me and snuggled up to me on the sofa. A ten-year-old was now looking after my crumbling body.

In suffering,
Jess

13th July 2006

Dear Bug,

My body hurts as I lie crumpled on the sofa, trying to fathom what is happening to me. How am I going to continue to learn? Learning is all I know and now I can barely read without the words jumbling up into a mess. My brain is like a scrambled egg. The most horrendous thing is now they need proof that I am off school with good reason, so the truancy officer came to see us.

She arrived and her eyes widened whilst she watched my pain-riddled legs shaking uncontrollably. It was clear she wasn't expecting this. What even is this? I can no longer tell. I have lost a lot of weight and it's clear that there is something wrong, yet nobody is here to fix it.

The truancy officer's words utterly shocked me. She explained to Mum that, having seen me, drastic measures need to be put in place. My decline means that going to a mainstream school is not an option anymore.

As I watched her, my eyes started to burn from the normal sunlight. My fingers felt like they were pieces of rock. I had not been expecting the devastating news that I will now have to leave the school that has been my home for the past three years, to leave my friends. Now, I have to start a 'hospital school.'

I have always believed that I am going to get better and go back to school. To suddenly find out that, in fact, I will not be going back to my school and they can only *hope* that I will be able to do more GCSEs. What's happening? Why does no one have an answer?

Jess

1st September 2006

Oh Bug,

I am so confused by all these symptoms. I honestly can't believe that people honestly believe that this disease doesn't exist! If they could only see me now!

The light is scalding my eyes and causing headaches. At first, I only slightly noticed it but, as the days have passed, the curtains became closed more and more, even in daylight. Nowadays, there is just a slit of light peeking through the curtains throughout the day. Sound pierces my brain to the extent that I have to wear earplugs. The television is too much. I can no longer get up onto my top bunk so little Becky has let me borrow her bed. I would love to talk to you more, Bug, but alas, thinking is too much.

Jess

15th October 2006

Dear Bug,

The room is pitch black, my body aches and I can just about crawl to the bathroom with help. When I do that, it takes over half an hour to move just two metres, as I have to heave my body, pushing with all my might. Good God, what is happening?

Embarrassingly, Tom (yes, my brother!) has to help me, alongside Mum. There is no 'downstairs' anymore. That is a distant memory, a place I desperately need to get back to, but how?

Another virus has infiltrated my weakened body. This time it is in my throat. I can't swallow without being in agony: the energy to eat is fast eluding me. I'm caught in a vicious circle. I know I need to eat but am so limited. Both eating and drinking give horrific pain, which means I'm totally drained by it. I have no energy to chew on food and have lost a vast amount of weight as a result. Having entered the vicious circle, it is incredibly hard to see a way out. I am down to soft food and ice cubes to suck on to try and make sure I get some form of nutrients.

The exhaustion oozes out of every pore in my body and, with every small movement, I can feel its presence hovering over me. *What can I do?* I ask myself, as my bewildered family work hard to help me.

I've got to write this Bug, I have to show someone what is happening so they will do something. It seems that only you are listening.

Louise comes round every week. She is a show-stopping, beautiful brunette, short and slim with gorgeous, big, brown eyes. I have known her all my life. She's watched my decline and has helped my fight by being a friend. We lie on the floor together on a double duvet. She is a part of my life, simply by visiting. . . by being there. . .

Jess

At first, we did try to keep something going to provide some normality for poor little Becky. I would go downstairs for my food in the evening until one day (Nick was visiting on this day) my body couldn't hold itself up. I couldn't swallow the soft fish pie that Mum had made specially. I fell apart inside as my body swayed. Tom picked me up and took me back to my room. I lay on my bed, the candle providing the only light between Nick and me.

6th November 2006

Dear Bug,

Every time I need to use the bathroom, I have to have help. I hate having to admit this.

Tell me what to do and I will God-damn-well do it! I am raging inside. Do they not realise what an important year this is? Help me! Please? Yet there is nothing they can give me for the stabbing pain and the weight loss. My family are tortured by my decline, with no answers. Thud. Thud. Thud. I can barely swallow. Energy scuppering. Why can't the professionals see?

CHAPTER THREE

Welcome to My World
Exhibit 'A' at the Museum

Fourteen days later
The noise in the hospital bay boomed through my sound-sensitive ears as the lights scorched my eyes. The smell of the hospital food came wafting into the bay, exhausting me further as my brain tried to identify each smell. Even the texture of the rough sheet hurt my skin that had become sensitive too. In my semi-conscious state, everything became a blur and piecing it all together was such an effort.

I remember asking for help from the doctors, as my body steadily deteriorated, but this was their only answer. A hospital. No explanation or knowledge of what to do next. It must have been a sorry state of affairs to see the teenager, who used to be so full of life, taken down the stairs of her house on a stretcher. Her face as sickly pale as the sheets covering her.

*

I remember the day before that. Dad had carried me to the car; I was a dead weight and I hadn't sat up in weeks. When we arrived at the hospital, Dad sat me in the wheelchair he had borrowed from work and trundled me into the hospital along with Mum.

My appointment had finally arrived for physiotherapy. I'd been waiting for months for the appointment and my health had deteriorated so much that Dad had insisted that I went along, even though my body could no longer hold my weight. We needed answers. Dark glasses covered my eyes because the light was too much for them.

The physios wanted me to do hydrotherapy. I could barely move and couldn't even muster the energy to sit up straight, I was leaning on Mum as they told me this. Could they not see? How would hydrotherapy be possible when I had to be carried everywhere?

I sobbed into Mum's lap. "Please help me, but don't hurt me."

I had always believed that I was going to get better, because there was no other acceptable option, but this was torturous and humiliating. I cursed my body, before rolling over and vomiting, leaving my parents completely bewildered at all the information they had been told. That was all the medical team offered me for the future: hydrotherapy. I was desperate. A simple car journey had caused so much more deterioration. Was it even possible to get worse?

When we got home, they pulled me up the stairs to my bedroom, one step at a time. The pair of them were wondering what had happened to their beautiful little girl.

Mum looked in dismay at my deterioration in health. I turned to look her in the eye. With every ounce of strength that I had left, I whispered, "Don't... give... up... on... me."

With tears in her eyes, she looked deep into mine and whispered back, "Never."

The tears fell silently down her face, as she conjured up all the determination she could muster, before defiantly adding, "For as long as I live."

She held my hand. The world around us shattering into a million pieces.

I was slowly slipping down the staircase of health with no idea where the bottom was. I remember Dad kneeling by my side but, before he could even utter a word, I whispered, "I. . . need. . . need. . . help."

"It's coming, darling, hold on tight." He then called for an ambulance to come and get me.

*

The paramedics arrived to take me to the hospital, which I would come to think of as 'the museum.' Everyone around me, from doctors to nurses, didn't know what to say. They were incapable of comprehending how the condition M.E.— believed by some to stand for 'More Excuses'—had caused so much desperate disaster.

Yes, doctor, I thought, *it is real. You aren't seeing things.* Just that brief thought cost me dearly and I lay there, mute, not certain if I were alive or dead.

Then another doctor came in and stood by my bed. I couldn't understand his words, it was as if he was speaking a foreign language. My parents tried to relay what he said. The basic summary was that he didn't know. He didn't know what to do for a girl who could barely find the energy to swallow, who needed his help.

I needed to be weighed and the only way they could do that

was to hoist me onto a big set of scales. It was the most bizarre and unpleasant feeling imaginable. My head was spinning as I was lifted into the air and my legs began to shake violently. I could only groan to communicate the discomfort that was being caused. It was all I could do to stop myself being sick when the hoist lowered me down onto the scales.

I couldn't see the hospital bay for my vision had started to fail me. My eyes were just too weak. Tears streamed down my face from sheer embarrassment when I realised that I was now being hoisted onto a commode. To them, I was just a patient, a bed number. They had seen everything before so didn't understand how difficult it was.

Had they never been fifteen? It was the first time that I had completely lost my dignity. I hoped it would be the last time too. The next day had to be a better day—surely?

After the hoisting experience, the doctors came back to set me a ludicrous task: I was to drink six to eight bottles of the energy drink Ensure by that evening.

My parents tried to explain to the doctors that it was not that easy, that I had trouble swallowing, but it was to no avail. I tried so hard to get the drinks down me. They were disgusting and made me feel even more physically sick. I just kept trying. I believed they would make me better. I believed with everything I had that this was going to make everything okay because the doctor had set the task. I clung to the belief that doctors know what they're doing, don't they? Was I naïve or just hopeful?

The hospital wing got louder and louder as more children were brought onto the bay; my senses had already been on overload. I tried to sing a song in my head to drown out the wails from the poorly children but it was torturous.

Two visitors had come to see me. I couldn't tell who they were. They sat patiently by my bed, holding my hand and whispering.

Thank goodness, later that day I was moved into a much quieter side room, after my wonderful parents explained the situation to the nurse. I don't know what this new room looked like; my eyes remained closed. I was becoming even weaker, as I tried to sip on the Ensure.

I could just hear the whispers and smell Mum's distinctive perfume when she hugged me. Dad's voice was deep even when he whispered. I had managed just one Ensure.

I was told that the other two people from earlier had been my brother and sister. Becky and Tom had always been such a huge part of my life. My family meant everything to me, yet I couldn't even recognise them.

I had to get at least a bit better by tomorrow. Dad was staying over at the hospital with me. This became a ritual, one night Dad, the next night Mum.

That was the good thing about being on a Children's ward— somebody could stay over with you. The treatment had to work for my own sanity. How much longer could I continue like this?

CHAPTER FOUR

The Cry for Help

My second day in the hospital loomed over me, but the doctors' efforts were not enough to stop the mist of dehydration that fogged over my brain.

I was starving because I hadn't managed to drink any of the Ensure that was meant to give me the calories I needed.

People's words were comforting but incomprehensible. My brain felt strangely disconnected from my body. Maybe it was exploding? I was fighting the unknown, worsening as the hours went by. Even when you thought it could get no worse, there was further to go.

I could tolerate no food and barely any water orally. Speech—lost. Movement—lost. Nutrition—lost. Sensations—going. Too exhausted to even think complete thoughts.

*

Bug, from the emaciated me:

Where are you Bug? What? Why? How? Questions with no answers. . . Words with no sentences. . .

Body shutting down. . . yet so thirsty, so very sick, exhaustion, such terrible exhaustion. . . Still, I am holding. . . holding onto something, gripping onto life with all my remaining strength.

So much pain, so hungry, but sick. It's been months since my diagnosis of. nothing . No help. . . Need something. . . Something. . . Anybody. . . Please. Please. . . help me . . .

Imagination fading. Distant places, just swirling in confused manner. . . But still so bright. It hurts. . . Sound is loud. . . Body in torture. . . Holding on. . . Just holding on. . . to whatever force is still keeping me alive.

Mum's hand, then a gulp of water. . . Barely swallowing. Breathing is heavy. . . Mum's here. I choose to fight this, so am fighting it. . . Holding on. . . Just holding. . .

CHAPTER FIVE

My Guardian Angel

I felt heavy; my heels had begun to go red with the constant pressure from lying and unmoving in bed. The charge nurse looking after me, who also happened to be the ward manager, spoke to me, acknowledging that I was there.

"Not a well girl at all, are you love? We need to get this sorted. You can't go on like this."

This sounded like someone who was going to do something to ease my suffering, but she was going to have a fight on her hands, as she joined the frustrating 'wait and see' queue within the doctor's mindset. The same queue that my parents had joined much earlier, on my admission.

*

Every part of my body began to stop working; to even think was pushing the boundaries. I sat, locked inside my brain, as the M.E. Monster waged war.

It was like being in a room where there were hundreds of doors that all led to different neurological pathways and I could only watch as the doors began to close. The reality of what was happening vaguely passed through my mind but all my focus went to trying to fight on, to keeping going.

The last thing to go was my imagination. No thoughts passed, no imagery. I was simply a shell, no more and no less.

I closed my eyes to quietly soothe the shell. Instead of the usual darkness one sees with closed eyes, there was a white light illuminating my vision. It was bright and white yet it did not hurt at all.

Suddenly, I was hovering upright about a metre away from a bed. A man sat in the corner to my right and I recognised him as my dad; he was reading a book. Everything seemed slightly brighter, a powerful sense of stillness billowed into my being.

I looked over to my left and saw the girl occupying the bed. Her skin was a greyish white and her eyes were hidden behind dark glasses. There was such a contrast between her long, dark hair and her sickly, pale skin.

A voice was talking to me. I did not know what gender, or who it was, telling me it would be alright, but this magical state did not scare me and, to be honest, it didn't even cross my mind to wonder who it was. Instead, I just let it touch my inner being.

"It is going to be okay, Jess. It is going to be okay," the calm voice repeated.

Was this some sort of beautiful dream? I knew that couldn't be true because I could feel how real it was, yet I no longer had any sense of body weight. There was a feeling of peace: no fear or pain warping my body. Just simple, stunning peace.

The things that were so important in daily life—the date,

the day of the week and the time—in this moment, all those concerns simply fluttered away. I didn't even need to think of them. It is difficult to describe quite what this place was and how I felt connected to it because there are simply no words within the English Dictionary to describe it. It was a luxury to know someone was with me, that I wasn't on my own in this Limbo Land. Yet, I did not spare a thought for why this was so. I didn't need to.

"It is going to be okay, Jess, you are alright."

Dad kept looking over towards the bed, straight through me, the look of deep worry never escaping from his face. He had heard no grunt from the bed; no slight whimper had reached his hearing.

"You are okay, Jess, it is going to be alright."

It may sound ridiculous, but only then did I realise that it was my body in that bed, my body that my father was finely tuned to so as to hear any whisper or twitch within it. Yet, I was not currently in that body. This didn't scare me or change my feeling of peace. It was just a fact that I didn't need to be concerned with.

"It is okay, Jess."

This sensation could have lasted minutes or it could have lasted seconds, I would have known no difference. For the first time, I could actually see my side room on Sunshine Ward.

"It is okay, Jess. It is going to be okay."

Dad stood bolt upright, putting his book down, he picked up another object, which I couldn't see. He walked towards the bed, straight past me and leaned over the body. I tried to see but I needn't have done so; in that wonderful state of peace I had no concerns about the world around me.

Once more, I observed the strange stillness that filled this slightly brighter version of the darkened room, brighter yet not hurtful to my sensitive eyes. Then there was that voice again.

"There we go, Jess. It's not your time yet."

The next part happened so quickly, so incredibly quickly. A numb sensation moved my lips as if something was touching them.

Within a matter of moments, I returned to my body. I blinked to see Dad holding a drink bottle and opening my lips slightly with the nib to pour the water in. The exhaustion was back with a vengeance, alongside the aching and all the other symptoms. Again, I could barely even think.

It had been an out-of-body experience; it was the only possible explanation for what had happened. At the time, and for a good while afterwards, I didn't even try to find a reason. I have never been overly religious; I don't believe that one faith is right or one is wrong. I have always been taught to look for the real person and not to judge. So please feel free to make up your own mind about what happened in that hospital room, but after experiencing those events, it certainly made me wonder.

Before long, I was joined by both of my parents and there were rapid conversations going on between them and the ward manager. The doctors were still taking the approach of 'wait and see' but they were not there all the time.

I was gripping on with my entire being, even though it had been days since I had received a proper meal or fluids. It was at this point that the ward manager took charge of the situation.

"I will NOT watch a young girl starve to death on my ward," she said frustrated.

With that, she went against the doctors and went straight to the next stage which was feeding me manually through a nasal gastric (NG) tube, something that would finally sustain my fragile body.

According to my parents, the ward manager checked me over, tutting quietly. She gathered the things she would need whilst measuring the size and length of the tube. Mum then swiftly left before the procedure, leaving me with Dad, because she couldn't bear to see the discomfort that this invasive step would cause to her baby.

I was unaware of what was about to happen.

It just feels so abnormal to have a hard wire covered with plastic shoved up one nostril. When the tube reaches the top of the throat, you are told constantly to swallow as it is pushed further down. This was a huge problem for the nurse doing the procedure because I was already struggling to swallow. Your body retches constantly to get rid of the foreign body but that only pushes the tube back up again and it must go down, no matter how traumatic it is. A weakened body trying to vomit is not a pleasant sight.

Dad kept encouraging me, trying to soothe me.

Swallow. Swallow. Swallow.

My tummy disagreed with the tube as I'm sure anybody's would at first. Then I was sick, but luckily the tube stayed in situ.

I was limp and exhausted. The nurse had realised what needed to be done a long time ago. Although the doctors are ultimately in charge, the nurse was professionally accountable for her actions. She therefore went ahead with the procedure, which essentially saved my life.

As she scanned the mess that had been made by the doctor's inability to act, the nurse and my parents were all thinking the same thing: that tube should have been put down on day one not day three. Maybe then my health would not have declined to this extent?

The ward manager lowered her tone to say, with a sigh of relief, "Thank goodness, somebody up there has been looking after you."

CHAPTER SIX

Limbo Land

The ticking of machines awoke me from my quiet reverie. My hospital surroundings and distant places from my old life fell in and out of my vision but my body didn't move. Voices—was somebody there?

The alarm from a machine drilled in my head. *Please make it stop, make it stop!* It did without me having to verbalise my instruction. One blink and a blur of people filled my vision. They whispered hurriedly to me as my heart hammered. Then I was out.

A child's imagination is the most wondrous gift of endless entities. I climbed mountains in my rest, walked along the seashore as the waves cascaded against the cliffs. My mind took me to many places and I hung on to the imagery through the agony that crushed my body from fingers to toes.

"Jess, my baby? Mummy is here and your sister. We will look after you." Mum's voice swept into my dreamy state.

It's okay, Mum's here, I thought as I desperately tried to ride the storm.

I used to think of us as just an ordinary family but, once the M.E. Monster attacked, it changed us forever. My brother was a constant support at home and my sister would sit by my side. None of us had expected this latest turn of events despite the common knowledge that I had been declining in health for the past six months.

My family was a rock of support. Whilst their world crumbled, they remained resilient to what life threw at them. I wondered how on earth they were doing it. Too tired to think of possible explanations, I allowed my drifting state to see each family member beating drums to my steady heartbeat.

More moments passed; they could have been hours or even days—I just couldn't tell anymore.

"Sweetheart, hold on there, my darling girl, hold on," my Gran's comforting voice whispered urgently.

I was holding on. I opened my eyes to the room swaying like a ship at sea. Gran's face came into the light. Her sparkling smile with her twinkling blue eyes, always neat and tidy.

Gran was a second mum to me, very young at heart and fashionable. I wanted to talk to her, let her know that I was doing just that, I was holding on and I would keep going. Then the motion sickness took over and I was out again.

This time, my dreams literally started to swim. I was in an ocean of blue and my body was moving sinuously in a scuba-diving kit. I swam deeper and deeper, watching the stunning, vivid contrast of colours and the breadth of life. It was a place where fish swam in multi-coloured bursts, a place where you could never get bored.

"Jessica, my sweet? Let us go on adventures together! You remember our story we are writing? Together, we shall write a book and inform the world. People will queue up to buy it. Your dream, in fact, our dream—we will make it happen!" Gran said encouragingly.

I tried desperately hard to make her words form into intelligible sentences in my mind that I could understand; I finally thought I had managed it and then it was like somebody turned off the lights inside my brain. Gone again.

I was an inventor, a researcher, a model, and I travelled the world through my imagination. At that time, it was my only saving grace. I existed in a place I called Limbo Land, hovering between the conscious and the unconscious. I could hear my family talking to me, see images of them, yet I couldn't reply or make sense of what they talked about.

Previously, before any illness, I led a very active life. I was the netball captain at school. I enjoyed spending time with friends and family. Not one to play completely by the rule book, I enjoyed living a free life. Much of my time was spent reading stories. I loved being able to go into another world, just through the power of words.

Throughout that time, I excelled at school. I loved my brother and sister and had a close bond with them both in different ways. I'd had a story to tell, one full of interesting things. Now, though, if you looked into side room five and saw the motionless body of a ghostly white girl, you wouldn't imagine that could ever have been the case. I was nothing but a blank canvas.

As the NG tube started to give me nutrients, the hope that it would bring about a bounce back to health was soon extinguished. Square one seemed to like me. Limbo Land did too.

By taking so long to act, the doctors had left my body

hanging on the edge. I picked up on rare flashes of real life, which I tried to store in a memory pot. Nothing was clear; a hazy mist of exhaustion smothered me whenever I tried to push to the surface.

It won't stop me trying, I thought earnestly. *I'll just keep on trying*.

I didn't know that giving up was an option nor did I really know the meaning of failure, for I still bore the innocence of childhood, even at fifteen. Maybe this was an advantage. Most adults have seen the real world and are, as they frequently remind us, older and wiser and more cynical.

What day of the week is it? I wondered. It was on this day, when my words were eaten up and I was left motionless by the M.E. Monster, that somebody came and started to move my limbs. But, to me, it felt like they were lifting heavy boulders: I was a complete dead weight.

The agony was so immense that I started to cry, wishing that the pain would subside. Sharp, searing pain like electric shocks riddled me from the simplest touch against my skin. This was my first meeting with the physiotherapist, whom I went on to refer to as a physio-terrorist! It was always important to maintain my sense of humour; I meant no malice. My sense of humour became the only light in a darkened place. I was out again, back to desperately fighting to get to the surface.

I could no longer tell when I needed the toilet so regular hoists on to the damn commode were part of my daily routine. A catheter was a terrible intrusion, they said. So, instead, I spent all day trying to get to the surface and consciousness just to be hoisted up unceremoniously and to crash back underneath the surface afterwards. There were no tears anymore; I had no energy to think about those who were looking at me or to care that my dignity had been taken from me.

One day, the nurses and Mum had rolled my limp body over so they could fit the hoist sling. This simple manoeuvre alone was enough to make me feel dizzy but there was worse to come today. I heard the familiar sound of the hoist and imagined that it was a gigantic claw, like the ones in the arcade game where you try to pick up the toy. It was always a traumatic affair because it was difficult not knowing where you were or in what direction you were swinging. Once hoisted into the air, I would usually be guided over to wherever the commode was and plonked down onto it. I would sit, slumped against a friendly figure whom I just about recognised was Mum. And then out.

But this time, as my dead weight slipped unceremoniously through the hoist sling, urine went everywhere. Mum was desperately holding on to me whilst I groaned, suffering. Eventually, three nurses emerged to answer the utterly desperate shouts for help from the male nurse and Mum.

Once I was back in the bed, Mum entered into deep discussions over the hoisting situation.

"That cannot happen again! I mean, goodness, imagine what could have happened," she said tearfully. "There has to be another way!"

"When she is a bit better, we could try rolling her on to a bedpan?" the nurse suggested.

"There is no maybe about it, this is a must! We will have to use a bed pan, I am not watching that struggle again," Mum said shakily.

After that ordeal, I was in and out of Limbo Land for what felt like weeks. I had started to lose track of time.

My little sister sat with me with her blonde hair and blue eyes, who had been forced to grow up before Mother Nature intended. She went without the trusted guidance of my parents whilst they became Supermum and Superdad, darting from place to place on my behalf. She was a hard worker; I hoped that studying would bring a new life for her, take her away from all the worry and upheaval.

I was to learn that, every day after school, she sat by my bedside as a ritual until she was taken to another temporary 'home' with a friend or relative. It was a hard life, yet she never complained. Nor did she tell a soul the truth about how poorly I was for that would just confirm her greatest fear—making the thought that maybe I wasn't going to make it all—too real.

As my sister sat silently by my bedside again that day, the most harrowing truth was that Limbo Land did not even allow me to know she was there.

CHAPTER SEVEN

Bluebell Hill

Whilst I fought to stay conscious, the world around me changed frequently as different members of my family took over the duties of looking after me. I was unaware of the changes; it was all just a blur of images seen through my haze. The excruciating pain mixed with the thick suffocating blanket of exhaustion was all too much.

At these times, I would go to Bluebell Hill inside my head. It is a tranquil place in Kent that overlooks miles of countryside. I could feel the soft, dewy grass at my feet, saw the trees dancing a slow waltz with one another and heard the sweet birdsong drifting happily from the trees.

As I walked, the sun's glow kindly kissed my cheeks and I breathed in the scent from the wild rose bushes with their deep crimson blooms that grew along the track. There was a massive clearing on top of the hill where, for a moment, I felt on top of the world as the view went on. Fields, country lanes, towns, churches, all fell at my feet. It was a beauty to behold.

I used to walk along these same tracks with Gran before I became ill. There was great comfort in visiting places in my dreams. It was only at that point that I realise how privileged

I was to have experienced walking those tracks in real life. A privilege that most take for granted.

Back in the hospital room, I became acutely aware of my best friend, Nick, whispering a conversation to me. I thought about how hard it must be for everyone to have a one-sided conversation and I so wanted to join in. If only I could tell him that it was okay and that, one day, we would go to all the magical places he spoke about.

I focused on trying to involve myself in the conversation in some way but it was no use. My ruthless punishment for the effort of trying to escape the M.E. Monster was Limbo Land and more torturous symptoms. I would still persist though. There had to be a way.

Those friends who were allowed to see me were distressed by what they saw. They hadn't realised how much I had deteriorated whilst they had been carrying on with their lives. The world doesn't stop spinning to wait for people like me to jump back on the ride. It carries on. I was left in space.

Everybody had heard about cancer and heart attacks but no one had heard of M.E. Why was this? I knew a girl with M.E. once but all I was told was that she got tired. Never did I question it or think about what she was going through.

ME is not merely about getting tired. It angers me that people believe this. If I could have got up and moved, I would have done so. I couldn't wait for the time when that would be possible and I could say that I'd beaten the M.E. Monster. At that time, it was nothing but a dream because every day was a battle.

Over the weeks that passed, more people came to see me, or rather to see what had been left behind by the tornado that had blitzed my entire being. I tried desperately to converse and fell deeper into Limbo Land.

Keep at it Jess, I encouraged myself. *Your day will come.*

That day did come. Nick sat by my side once more. He was a tall, dashingly handsome, young man who, despite being in his A-Level year, took the time out to come and see me every week. It was nice that he made such an effort. I wanted him to know that I too was making the same effort, even though it may not have been so visible.

"Are you depressed, Jess?" he quietly murmured.

Oh Nick, why would I be depressed? I am a warrior! I am fighting this! I must show him that I'm not depressed, but how? I shook my head inside and felt my head move slightly from side to side.

"Oh my God, Jess, you are hearing me! You ARE hearing me!"

The excitement was clear in his voice. I nodded my head and felt a very slight jerk of a nod pushing my head forwards just as Mum turned round. With tears in my eyes, I watched the joy in theirs.

"You are doing it my baby. Oh darling, you are doing it!" Mum said excitedly.

I nodded again, although this time it didn't translate to physical movement. Then I was out.

I fell into dizzy spells of sickness.

"Go to Bluebell Hill, Jess," I heard Mum say as she held my hand.

The distant voices that drifted in whilst I dozed in and out of different places in my mind palace were of some comfort. I sat on Bluebell Hill whilst the M.E. Monster growled and groaned at my victory. My insides were seizing up but I firmly told myself that it couldn't take away what I had managed; my dormant body was waking up.

No! I thought desperately. *No one can take this moment away from me.* My brain growled and snarled in sheer agony. *Take me to Bluebell Hill*, I prayed. I could smell the soft grass at my feet. I was there with the scrumptious scent of Gran's perfume sweet in the air, there in the safe haven I had made.

CHAPTER EIGHT

Songbird

Lying in a bed, unable to communicate, clearly had many drawbacks. People couldn't fathom how I remained so positive. Even through the pain and the exhaustion, I managed to form a kind of smile via a twitch at the nurses. Giving up was not an option.

Being bedridden was my reality—there was no getting away from the fact. Therefore, for my own sanity, I needed a coping mechanism. I would think about the book that Gran and I were going to write one day, when I was better. This nurtured a deep hope for a future beyond ME.

I had been tested for so many different conditions to make sure that I was being treated for the right one. I didn't know if I should be leaping for joy that nothing else was found or daunted by the scale of the battle against this misunderstood condition that I now had to face.

ME is a neurological disease that is known for causing a multitude of severe symptoms affecting patients to different degrees. Some people can still work, and others on the more severe spectrum can be so debilitated that they become housebound or completely bedbound. It currently has no scientific cure or particular treatment that works definitively on each patient.

Commonly used treatments are Graded Exercise Therapy, and Cognitive Behavioural Therapy. These have been proven not to be entirely successful but there is no other treatment available.

In my case I was at the very severest point. However, my parents did not want to scare me, so I did not know the true extent of the disease or the fact there was a chance I would not get better.

Before becoming ill, I had been a music fanatic, playing instruments, singing and listening to music too—a little songbird. I had a rich and diverse palette of musical influences, from Mozart to Coldplay.

Tom had taken me and Mum to a Coldplay concert in 2005. It had been one of the highlights of my life! Hearing thousands of people singing 'Fix You' and connecting with one another for that one moment in time, was enchanting.

Maybe one day I will write a song that people feel they have the same connection to, I had thought. I often visited this memory whilst I was ill and couldn't help but grin inside.

I started singing to myself, hearing the music in my head. I couldn't even bear the sound of the nurses talking, so real music was utterly out of the question. Within my internal world, I could play any song at any moment, as if I were a DJ in charge of a disco.

The lyrics to 'Fix You' by Coldplay had a powerful meaning to me. They spoke of going home and fixing people. Oh, how I wanted to go home and not be in this hospital bed. I needed fixing, not mentally, but physically. I would imagine that I was visiting a garage which sold different body parts and a new brain was on order. If only.

The month had ticked by as we headed into December and I was still the same, always praying that tomorrow would be a better day, one in which I made some progress. The doctors still weren't giving me any medication to make me better, only to try to relieve my pain.

I couldn't understand why there had been very little research done on this dreadful illness that affects so many. *What's that strange gurgling in my stomach?* I remember hearing the sound but I couldn't connect it to a feeling.

Mum had told me that they were going to stop feeding me through the NG tube all the time and instead, they were going to mimic me having 'meal times' (certain times in the day where I would be fed through the tube). I still couldn't work out what that noise meant though. Then out.

Through the patient support of my family and friends, my state of consciousness was slowly improving. Urgent whispering would wrench me away from Limbo Land. I'd open my eyes to a swarm of stimuli; the light, the sounds, the person standing over me. I wondered if people understood how imposing it is having someone towering over you? I suppose they don't or they wouldn't do it.

The first time Louise had visited she just sobbed, whilst her mum chatted nervously to me. I couldn't understand what she was saying—by the time I pieced one part together, she was already murmuring about something else. The sheer effort of trying to understand sucked the energy out of me as if it were a mosquito sucking my blood. I fought against Limbo Land, I really did, but as I tried I seized up in agony. Then the exhaustion strangled me and I was out; the flick switch said so, I had no choice.

I had rediscovered some form of movement. I practised my nodding and head shaking but the movements didn't keep up with the conversation and caused some awful situations. The 'Yes and No Game' has a time and a place. The time and the place were not Sunshine Ward!

For those of you not familiar with the 'Yes and No Game,' I shall briefly explain the rules. If you don't understand the question being put to you, you still reply; you either nod or shake your head. I liked to play the game because it made people feel they were getting a response to their whispered questions.

One day, Nick was sitting by my bedside, chatting in whispers to me. I decided to play the 'Yes and No Game' because I felt bad that I could not concentrate on his conversation and I so wanted to be able to join in. I really did. But, again, I was being prevented from doing so by the M.E. Monster.

Nick continued to chat and every so often would look up at me, trying to see through my dark glasses, to see the eyes that used to tell him stories just by looking at them. I would hastily choose either 'yes' or 'no' and before long, to my horror, he burst into tears. I didn't know what to do, I had never seen Nick cry. What on earth could have upset him so much?

He reached out and held my hand. I tried with all my might to show him that I was there for him. Much to my delight, the slightest flicker of a squeeze pushed its way down my arm. Most importantly Nick felt it and knew I was there.

"How long have you known?" he asked me tentatively.

I stayed stock still, not knowing what or how to respond, utterly confused by the situation.

Fortunately, Mum and his mum came in at that point and saw his tears. He managed to tell them what was wrong. It turned out that, through my 'Yes and No Game,' I had managed to tell him that I was dying from an unknown condition, secondary to M.E. Shit! That was a dangerous game to play.

"Don't ever do that to me again," an emotionally wrecked Nick whispered into my ear after Mum had explained the misunderstanding.

He needn't have worried, for I didn't intend on ever seeing my best friend in such a state again. The 'Yes and No Game' was banned!

CHAPTER NINE

Psycho Woman

The level of misunderstanding about M.E. was ludicrous. My very existence baffled people—how could a child be this ill and not be depressed? All the blood tests had come back negative so they assumed it must be something psychiatric.

How on earth could I reach out to people and tell them that I was still fighting? I was still waging war against this little known condition when my own body prevents such efforts? In fact, why was it even necessary for me to be wasting precious energy trying to find a way to explain what the medical professionals should already know?

Weeks felt like months. As we reached Tom's twenty-first birthday in December, I wanted to write him a card. As this was physically impossible, I needed to try my hardest to dictate the shortest possible message to tell him how much I loved him.

It's funny how we overuse those words, yet they are the most important words we can say. I slowly whispered my code, using just the first syllables or letters of words, to communicate my blurred thoughts. No matter how quiet and incomprehensible the sounds were, I was determined to do it.

"I. . . I," I whispered to Mum.

"Yes baby, yes, I got it!" she said encouragingly.

"L. . . l. . . l. . . luf. . ."

"Love?"

"Y. . . ya. . . you," I stammered as I pushed my body to do as I willed with all my might.

I was immensely proud of myself. Mum was bursting with pride. Her little girl was winning against this M.E. Monster. I had said three muffled words, even if most people wouldn't have understood. As I swirled with joy, exhausted from my efforts, I slowly fell out of consciousness again and the world continued on.

Later on, I could hear Tom's voice. I couldn't make out his exact words or the conversations that were going on around me amongst the small gathering of my family. I opened my eyes to the blurry haze that engulfed my vision. I tried to focus on the shapes that moved and got dizzy with motion sickness from moving my eyes too quickly. *Was this what it felt like to have a massive hangover?*

I could make out the shape of Tom, the birthday boy, coming towards me. He kissed my forehead and whispered the words so only I would hear amongst the hustle and bustle going on around.

"I love you, Jess. Always remember that."

I smiled at the words. Our connection was glowing again. That was my brother, my brother who I had managed to speak to in a muffled new form of language.

Not long after my family left, I was sick and sick and sick, as the M.E. Monster ate me up. It felt like the angry sea crashing against the rocks I was clinging to; all my effort went into simply learning how to hold on. My eyes felt like they had nails scratching down them, my eye sockets continuously pummelled. I could bear this, though, because I held onto the thought that I had just made my first impact on the world. I had re-discovered my voice.

As Christmas approached, the psychiatrist came to see me. It was tedious but necessary.

"It must have been a hard life for you," she said.

No, in fact it was quite the opposite–when I was well!

There was an uncomfortable silence, as I was angered by her words.

"You shared a room, didn't you? That must have been awful, not having your own space. All children should have their own space."

Obviously, she was not very aware of the normality of family life.

The frustration. As much as I tried, I couldn't say anything. The pure effort was too much, the pain unbearable, the brain fog smothered my words, as they attempted to leave my mouth.

The eerie silence spread into every corner of the room. All that could be heard was the machine, as it pushed more substances into my gurgling stomach. I clung on, trying desperately hard not to sink beneath the surface–I needed to hear what she was going to say. Come on body! Come on! But the switch flicked and the light went out.

My heart hammered in my chest. Limbo Land took hold of me. Voices of people coming in and out of my room echoed in my burning head. It was all I could do just to metaphorically hold my hands to my head whilst the wrath of the M.E. Monster took hold of me. It really didn't like being told what to do.

The psychiatrist observed as I fell into a practically unconscious state. It was easy to tell when I was in LimboLand because I could not interact at all. The M.E. simply switched my system off into nothingness.

*

Christmas 2006 was nearly upon us. I knew this because, for the brief moments I forced my eyes to open, I could see a small Christmas tree and other decorations in my room. There was also an abundance of teddies and posters, so I could see something other than those all-too-familiar four walls.

Nick had been visiting me weekly but he came in early this time with a Christmas present for me. He wouldn't let me wait and have the gift on Christmas day.

"Babes, you are in desperate need of these. I can't allow my babes to look like this in hospital!"

He pulled out the gift and to my surprise it had the words Dolce and Gabbana on the lid.

"These are a necessity. If you are going to hide those beautiful eyes from me, then I want you looking stylish."

The gleaming D&G sunglasses looked at me screaming, 'Wear me!'

I had never owned anything that was designer, and as I allowed Nick to take off my old sunglasses and replace them with these beauties, I couldn't help but feel lost in gratitude to him. I rubbed my lips together, which meant 'hug' but Nick wasn't up on the code language. He just smiled and held my hand.

"That's better. I mean how were we ever going to get you a man if you had those ugly glasses on?"

*

My family were being forced into having family therapy to deal with the crisis. They all loathed the very mention of it; even the fact that it meant skipping school couldn't bring a smile to my sister's face. Instead, after every session, my darling little Becky would sob silently in the corner of my room.

How can you ask a twelve-year old, in front of both of her parents, to tell the mediator which parent she loves more? Unbelievable! This was the kind of support they gave my family who were willingly caring for me 24/7.

Anger brewed and bubbled inside me. *Just keep fighting, Jess, it's your only way out of this mess*, I thought.

Christmas came and went, and I vowed that I would never spend a Christmas in that state again. I had to lay there on my own, in silence, because the sound of Christmas carols was simply too much for my ever-so-delicate ears.

Every Christmas, as a family, we used to decorate the tree together and watch *The Snowman* on Christmas Eve. On this particular year, Becky did the tree alone whilst I could only imagine myself there with her.

There just wasn't enough time to do everything in my superhero parents' schedules, especially with Dad working full time and Mum being in the hospital with me most of the day, to do all the usual Christmas traditions.

My gran held my hand and made everything okay. She

spoke in hushed whispers. I couldn't grasp all of what she was saying but I clung onto the dream we had together.

"You are going to keep fighting this, Jess, I know you all too well. Can you promise me something?" she asked quietly.

The vigorous nodding I was doing in my head translated into a slight jerk.

She continued, "Will you start planning our book? We will write it together. I need you to decide on the characters; I need you not to give up because we will never give up on getting you through this."

I held onto every word and then slowly drifted out.

Before I was ill, we would spend most weekends at Gran and Pops' house, playing endless games with my cousins, creating imaginary worlds in the garden. Anything was possible.

As I grew older, I chose to spend more time with Gran. We loved to shop until we dropped, then to sit by a welcoming open fire and eat her famous stew, as the flames flickered and danced. I used to visit those comforting memories with great joy in my quiet reverie.

I planned the book that I would write with her. I was reminded of Becky's face with tears streaming down her cheeks because of the psychiatrist's regime, so the first character had to be, 'Psycho Woman'. The lady who wouldn't leave me alone and was making matters increasingly worse. The pantomime villain.

She wanted my family to be less involved in my life because, in her opinion, a teenage girl should be rebelling against her parents. The truth was far from that: I wanted nothing more than to cuddle up in my mother's love. I yearned to get better and I couldn't care less about rebelling.

The community psychiatric nurse who I was being forced

to see was amusingly called Dodo, so I immediately renamed her, 'Dodo the Extinct'! She would sit in my room trying to be what she considered cool but failing miserably with every attempt. She seemed oblivious to the main problem: whilst she was busy trying to be hip, hop and happening, I was stuck in a bed unable to move or speak.

The Christmas song 'Walking in the Air' now reminds me of the week before Christmas, when Dodo the Extinct had arrived in my hospital room with her blonde bob, high heels, multiple scarves and coat. I had been thinking of the song because it had always been a Christmas favourite.

I wasn't just tired, I was completely comatose, yet still she insisted on staying an hour so we could have 'me time.' Apparently, I could do anything I wanted in this time: just lie there in silence or talk or play games, even though these were things I couldn't do. She was trying to get something out of me, talking to me like I was just playing at this not-talking lark. As if, for one moment, that was my choice.

I begged my body to speak every single second of every single day. The more I begged, the more incredibly ill I became. I couldn't even flicker an eyelid, the energy required was just too much, but the yearning never stopped. It was criminal of her to think that this was anything other than a real disease. People don't just suddenly lose everything on purpose.

Flick.

The light switched off again. Whatever thought I had been grasping for disappeared and I started to walk on the air in dreams, as my body shook uncontrollably. I believe the Extinct One continued to chat on and on before leaving. Sadly, I heard nothing.

Psycho Woman continued to come and visit me every two weeks, whilst Dodo the Extinct came every week. They both sat in my side room in silence, wrote a few notes then tried to change my treatment plan to no avail.

Despite feeling a bit lost in the system, as I waited for a bed in a more experienced hospital, at least I wasn't having any psychiatric medication forced onto me. They couldn't prove that I was depressed and this was a huge plus. The doctors simply didn't know what to do. To be honest, I don't think Psycho Woman knew either.

I decided that I needed to do something proactive: the past few months had been a waste and I would not let this condition take away every aspect of my life. There had to be something I could do.

Maybe something that will help the book, I thought, and then it dawned on me: I would continue the diary I had started before I became ill. The one called 'Bug', as it was a fly-on-the-wall account of every day.

I would re-start it on New Year's Day, which would give me time to plan my first entry! The question was, how on earth would I be able make my entries, written or spoken, if I could barely even mutter my name?

CHAPTER TEN

The World According to 'Bug'

With New Year's Eve fast approaching the only plan to help get me better was to get specialised help, as this was just a general hospital. Did these people not realise that I was wasting valuable moments of my life?

I was meant to be doing my GCSEs and I couldn't even attend the hospital school I had enrolled in before becoming hospitalised. They were ready to set up a special one-to-one tutor for me and the opportunity was going to waste. I wouldn't allow time to just continue passing without finding something to do. Not anymore.

I had waited long enough for the medical profession and they had done nothing except stand around looking puzzled.

I was also getting bogged down by the psychiatrists who had to put their two pennyworth in to explain why I wasn't getting better as quickly as the doctors had hoped. You see, this was the problem: the medics were oblivious to the tiniest of changes that were like miniature miracles to me. I had managed to squeeze my best friend's hand a month ago and code three words to my brother, for goodness sake! Wasn't this cause for celebration?

There was no better time to re-discover Bug. I had to come up with a way to code to my parents, so that they could write down what I wanted to say. It involved a lot of guesswork and whispers of half-words that my parents would make into whole words, checking with me that they were correct before writing them into Bug.

I was still here; I hadn't died or gone into a deep coma. I was simply blocked from communicating with the outside world by a neurological condition. We had to find a way to show these professionals that I wasn't just an inert body—that I had an active mind and could make decisions.

I spent all day coming up with the sentence that I wanted to write, that I wanted people to see and hear. It was important that people knew there was still a person in side room five; I think sometimes this was forgotten. After much deliberation, I came up with the first line.

"Hmm. . . Hmm," I uttered a soft cry to let Mum know I was ready to begin. "L. . . L. . . loo. . . ka."

Mum stared at me, intently trying to comprehend the sounds before she whispered, "Look, darling one?"

My head jerked into a nod before continuing, "Ooo."

No, no that is not what I mean; I mean 'who', dammit!

I moved my head slightly to the side, indicating it was wrong. Mum then went through words that were similar to the sound.

"Who-z. . . Ba-ck!" I slurred.

"Look who's back! Well done, my darling, well done. Rest now and we shall do some more soon," Mum whispered.

I rested, both elated and worn out by my efforts. Finally, my prayers were being answered.

It was a slow journey but every day I would talk to Bug.

It often took the whole day to make one entry. My parents painstakingly listened to each sound I made and rejoiced in the breakthrough, the step toward recovery, that no doctor could deny.

JANUARY

10th January 2007
Dear Bug,

Look who's back! The World According to Bug seems a suitable name for this part of my life. Each word is chosen with great attention to detail and it's my parents' fault if anything is wrong! I'm only kidding. They are the light of my life, just like Becky and Tom, Pop and Gran. I'm really very lucky!

12th January 2007
Dear Bug,

I love the decoration of my room. Have you seen the picture of Orlando Bloom and Johnny Depp in *Pirates of the Caribbean*? One word: FIT! What a wonderful thing to wake up to. These nurses, they think I can't hear. They talk to Mum as if I'm not here, or don't talk at all! It would be nice to be included. The next nurse or doctor who tells me that I haven't been trying, I will telepathically scream this at them, "You don't realise what enormous effort is put into everything I do, even though to you it seems like nothing!"

15th January 2007
Dear Bug,

My NG tube came out in the night. I awoke to the nurses

removing it. They must have made a mistake in handover (when the shift changed), because they blamed me for pulling the tube out whilst I was asleep. I can't move for Christ's sake! Laughable, don't you think? It was pretty gross. They pulled the tube away, then put it on the dusty side table. Mum told me they then put the same tube down the other nostril. Grim. That's why I can smell sick. Sterile my arse.

17th January 2007
Dear Bug,

I'm getting ready to write *the* book with Gran. We always said we would write a novel one day, so I think about it now whenever the agony in my body makes me restless. I'm trying my best, Bug, because I don't think the doctors here live with much hope. I'm going to be better and walking in no time— once I get to this specialised hospital.

I know there have been discussions about me being moved to a medical unit that is specifically for M.E. sufferers. I call it The Promised Land. I have to be sixteen before I go so only a couple more months to wait I hope. It does seem pretty endless.

I want to be doing my GCSEs and going to school. I guess some things you have to wait for.

FEBRUARY

1st February 2007
Dear Bug,

I love seeing my friends even though they go all silly and don't really talk—unlike my best friend Nick. He likes to talk to me so much that I don't know what is going on, but that is just Nick! Even though I don't go to school anymore, Nick likes to keep me up to date on what is happening. I suppose I need to keep up with the gossip somehow. The rest of you need to talk to me guys! I may not be able to reply but I like to try to listen. Just, easy does it!

4th February 2007
Dear Bug,

Something feels wrong but the doctors aren't taking it seriously. They have found blood in my stool and I can't believe they are blaming it on constipation. My tummy hurts and I can feel a sharp stabbing pain. Ouch!

(My parents took this entry to the doctor and nurses.)

6th February 2007
Dear Bug,

Well, we found out what was wrong: my tummy is bleeding internally. The nurse was using a syringe to aspirate the NG tube and it filled with sticky red blood that went everywhere. This is not helpful for my plans to get back to shopping at Bluewater shopping centre in the future. Daydreaming is all I can do. I visualise myself there with my friends, with Nick, living it large to make up for all the missed time. I hate wasting time; it's not in my nature. Please help me get better.

8th February 2007
Dear Bug,

I've started to dream the day away so I'm no longer sure which memories are dreams and which are real memories. Very odd indeed! You would think I'd be bothered by my Dad's atrocious snoring that keeps the whole ward awake— not just me. But you see, I need my parents here. What if I need help? And there are no nurses available? I don't like being alone in a place that is not my home, even though it feels like I've been here forever.

11th February 2007
Dear Bug,

The physio-terrorist really doesn't have a sense of humour. Come on, you've got to laugh otherwise you'll cry, and what help would that be? I have a t-shirt that says: PHYSIO-TER-RORIST ALERT!!

Dad made the t-shirt. It's a joke but she didn't find it funny.

I always do my physiotherapy even if I'm barely able to think whilst my limbs are being moved. I'm sure she hurts me intentionally when she tries to sit me up and increase the angle every week, whether I'm ready or not. It's agony and it makes me sick. The room spins and then I'm ruined for days. I believe it is called graded exercise but it really doesn't seem to achieve anything.

The t-shirt was a nice change from wearing pyjamas. The pyjamas made me skin ache but I can't stand hospital gowns.

The nurses would laugh at all the different tops I wore on different days. It gave me an identity; I was not just a bed number.

12th February 2007
Dear Bug,

I've been in hospital for three blooming months officially today. I've got to make plans for my sixteenth birthday; at the very least, I want to be at home. I can't believe I will be reaching sweet sixteen. Plans for a party are already under way. I don't have time to be ill! If there are any doctors reading this, please help me!

MARCH

5th March 2007

Dear Bug,

Do you know what it's like to not even know your own name? It's strange, I don't like it, but Limbo Land was hard on me today because I am trying so hard with moving and eating. I had a bit of ice cream earlier but I really didn't like the student nurse who fed me. She said how much she pitied me and tried to force me to eat more ice cream. Then she moved the sticky tape that holds my NG tube to my face and that made it less sticky. I fell asleep and went into this whirlwind of feeling sick from the ice cream.

The hospital are forcing Mum to leave me more now that they have installed a baby monitor to pick up my small groans. This means that they want me to start having less time with them and even more nights on my own. I don't like this idea.

The sticky tape came off because it was loose and the tube started to edge out of my nose ever so slightly, but this soon progressed into mayhem. As the tube slipped out more, I could feel and taste the milk it was feeding me running down my throat. It's so strange being able to taste something you haven't actually eaten. I wept, I groaned, yet nobody came. It was horrible but I was saved by the bell when the machine's alarm went off.

7th March 2007
Dear Bug,

It is the return of Psycho Woman, the psychiatrist determined to prove her theory that I am depressed. She has been gone for ages but now she has returned and is trying to ruin everything.

Finally, after four months of just waiting for The Promised Land (the specialist hospital unit for people with ME) to come and assess the suitability of me going to them, they agreed to take me on. However, now everything is up in the air again. I think I should try and tell a funny joke and maybe that will finally convince her that I am NOT depressed or wanting to be this sick either. I mean, come on, who would actually want this?

10th March 2007
Dear Bug,

My joke must have worked and she has so far been leaving me alone. Thank goodness! She apparently read you, Bug, and admitted that I was quite clearly not depressed. Why do these doctors need to be told so many times?

11th March 2007
Dear Bug,

This will be my last entry for a while. I will return to you when I'm better and ready to live my dreams. Apparently, the doctor from The Promised Land said I shouldn't be wasting my time doing a diary because it is exerting too much energy. I never thought of you like that. I think of you as my key to the outside world, to finding my voice and improving my speech.

But they must know better so I shall do what they say because all I want is to be better.

See you soon x

Bug was a huge boost to my health. It got me practising my speech and slowly making the sounds more audible. I could only imagine that the doctors from The Promised Land Hospital had something momentous to replace it with, some form of therapy that would help me, but the void was filled with nothing. Nothing but loneliness and lots of it too.

All I could think was that the health professionals must know better than me; they were there to make me better. Even though I had been saying it for months with no results, I still believed that they would. Doctors always had the answers. I truly believed that.

CHAPTER ELEVEN

Don't Panic

I could feel the bars on my bed; they rattled like chains that were pinning me down. Although accustomed to these little noises, I was uneasy today. I was uneasy because, as the door closed on side room five, I was completely alone with no way of getting help. It marked the first step in the new regime that had been set out by the 'visitors' to try and get me used to how it would be in the new hospital.

The 'visitors' came from The Promised Land. I was going to be transferred to the specialist unit when I turned sixteen. In the same way as I made side room five a part of Sunshine Ward, even though it was actually part of an acute medical hospital, naming things made them familiar to me, friendlier and less frightening. It was these names that I would use, one day, when I wrote my book with my gran.

Under the new regime, I was only allowed to see Dad for five minutes in the evening and Mum was allowed in to give me a wash at midday. That was going to be my only contact with them. Not even privacy was permitted, as their visiting time would also be recorded on the baby monitor. No siblings, no friends, no Nick. No more Bug either.

If it is going to make me better then I will do it, I thought, for failure was not an option.

The people from The Promised Land had set out this plan. It was our understanding that the top doctor at The Promised Land made people with M.E. better.

My family's usual strength of character was being tested beyond all measure. Being forced to leave their desperately unwell daughter—it must have felt to Mum as though she were having her heart ripped out every time she closed that door.

The fear that nobody would answer my calls for help on the baby monitor haunted her to the very core. I could see the agony in her eyes when she was told the news about the new regime, the constant stabbing to her heart as she tried to explain to me what was going on.

Dad had taken the news wearily. Though it pained him, he decided to go with what they demanded, for the experts from The Promised Land must surely know my needs better than my parents. After all, the creators of the new regime were the experts.

So Dad hid his emotions. He had to accept that the only way for my brother and sister to get to see me now would mean him giving up his precious five minutes. It all seemed so wrong, so unjust, but he would go along with it because he loved me with all his heart, in that way only a parent can. I knew he hoped I would one day understand that they had been given no choice.

As two nurses started to wash me they tried to chat with me about the latest trends but they failed to make an impression on a girl who just wanted a warm hug from her family.

"Where's that bruise come from?" one nurse exclaimed, looking at my knee. "What have you been up to?"

I smiled, not having a clue how a bruise could appear from nowhere. Once they had got me clothed, they rolled me over and saw my arm. I had been vaguely aware of it throbbing quietly in the background, just another mild distraction amongst all my other discomforts.

"Oh my God, there's another one! But wait a minute. . ." The nurse placed her hand on my upper arm where the mysterious bruise apparently was. She suddenly looked aghast and she whipped her hand away, as though my skin had scalded her.

Horror-stricken, she mumbled, "There's a lump. I can feel it."

The mood in the room changed within a split second. For some reason, unknown to me, panic erupted like lava from an active volcano.

That lump must mean something, I thought, *and something sinister at that.*

Before I had time to continue this macabre chain of thought, the other nurse had rushed to feel my arm. With the same grim and horrified look that had adorned the first nurse's face she hurried from the room. When she returned, she was not alone—a nursing sister followed her in. An alien with green and purple spots would have got less curious and anxious attention than I was receiving.

The Sister touched the area and nodded, at which point one of the nurses started to wipe away tears. The Sister hugged them both and thanked them for spotting it.

"You've done the right thing, love," she said to the visibly shaken nurse who had spotted the lump. She then turned to me and crouched down as she held my hand. "Alright darling, don't you worry, you are perfectly safe, I'm now looking after you." With that she flew out of the room.

What on earth was going on? This was madness! Nurses crying and hugging one another in front of a patient? I felt too poorly to consider the situation in more detail.

One of the nurses took my pulse and discovered that it was going at a scarily fast rate. Another nurse took my temperature which, it turned out, was raging.

"Are you nervous?" she asked timidly.

I firmly shook my head, even though to an onlooker it would have looked like a small wobble. I was not worried because I remembered that previously I had had an infection on that arm that had required antibiotics. I was, however, bemused at the commotion. There was little time to think before the next round of onlookers arrived at the door with the Sister, talking in hushed voices.

The two doctors, who appeared at my bedside, both wore worried expressions. Within less than a minute, they were on the phone, talking quickly. The Sister was carrying an ambig-uous-looking object under one arm as the crowd started to grow significantly in my room.

It had only been five minutes since the nurses had told the Sister about the lump they had discovered and yet another doctor entered my little world. This time it was the chief consultant, the lady in charge of the whole paediatric department. It must be serious business to draw her away from her office.

She came over with a magnifying glass, demanded that the room be made lighter and looked deeply troubled by what she saw.

"Good gracious, yes," she murmured to the other doctors.

"I didn't know what to do," confessed the nurse who had found the lump, still shaking.

"She needs to be on full observations, including her heart, and we need bloods, immediately."

I groaned at the pain caused by her prodding.

"Alright love, we will look after you, nothing to fear," she said directly to me, before confirming to the assembly that red bags would be necessary.

I knew that red bags meant they thought I had an infection serious enough that all my laundry would be placed in them and incinerated instead of being washed.

I felt like an exhibit, something that people came to gawp at. Never before had so many doctors arrived so quickly. It was mildly concerning that only now were they saying that they would look after me—shouldn't that have been the objective from the start?

Machines were being connected to me, a heart monitor amongst them! Why was there such concern? What on earth did they think I had contracted? It remained a mystery to me.

I was momentarily reminded of the film *The Hitch Hiker's Guide to the Galaxy*, which I had been to see before getting ill. The slogan written on the Guide's cover was 'Don't Panic,' which seemed highly appropriate for my current situation. I don't think these nurses had seen the film otherwise they would have remembered the most important thing—don't panic!

The pain increased in my throbbing arm. I was being checked every five minutes and this time, I was actually being checked properly, on the minute, so they must have suspected that something was seriously wrong. You see, I knew from my parents that in the world of medicine, time is quite a different matter to what it is to us mere mortals. Five medical minutes usually means half an hour, and twenty minutes means two hours, at least!

More nurses and carers came in and out of my room. Meanwhile, Dad strolled unawares into the midst of this pandemonium. His face dropped when he saw the machines and the carer who was sitting by my side. He collapsed into a chair and found my hand to give it a comforting squeeze before asking what on earth had happened.

When the five minutes normally allowed for his visit had passed, he did not budge but sat there expectantly. The doctor in charge returned and started talking in very hushed tones with Dad.

Dad explained to me that a blood test was necessary. I was acutely aware that he was leaving out details, the doctors did not want to scare me. They wouldn't be this concerned about just taking bloods.

In all the five long months that I had been in the hospital they had never, apart from the first day, done blood tests on me. Maybe this was a foolish oversight, considering I was on amitryptiline, a drug known for its alarming side effects.

The blood was far from easy to extract from my ravaged body, in fact it was nearly impossible. Once they had prised my arm out of its permanently contracted position so that it was straight, it was the head consultant who ended up taking the blood.

Dad stayed until the furore had calmed down. The medical staff didn't know what had caused the racing heart palpitations and raging temperatures but they weren't taking any chances this time. Nurses came round to do a neurological observation, whilst a doctor carried out similar checks as well.

This was the cue for Dad to quietly slip away, deep concern still etched upon the furrows of his forehead. In contrast, the nurse voiced her concerns out loud, then said something that was a revelation to me. It was my book in the making, the seed from which this would grow.

"Sorry, I'm going to need to see your eyes for a neurological examination," she said abruptly, wrenching my attention away from the emptiness left by Dad's departure. "I'll remove your glasses."

My eyes screwed up in response to the scalding light.

"I need them open please."

I quickly did as she said. For a brief moment, my eyes came face-to-face with their arch enemy—the light.

"Oh my goodness, that is the first time I've actually seen the colour of your eyes! I must be the only nurse to have seen your peepers in all the time you've been here!" she exclaimed.

How very true, I thought. *I am the Girl Behind Dark Glasses who nobody really sees. A title for a book I think, and what a title it will be.*

I resolved to tell Gran so she could start planning it! Yes, the windows to my soul were hidden behind dark glasses in a body that didn't work.

*

The night moved at a painfully slow rate due to all the observations being carried out whilst the heart monitor detected my constant racing heartbeat (or tachycardia, as the medical profession call it). The cold sweats were distracting, but the exhaustion was such that I couldn't even move my lips to whisper for help.

I was kept under close watch as dawn approached. The hospitality girls weren't even allowed to empty the bins in case they caught the suspected contamination.

It seemed to be time for ward rounds when suddenly a herd of doctors appeared in my room alongside Dr Lu, the so-called M.E. specialist who had no idea what to do with me in normal circumstances, let alone now that I had a lump on my arm. They all stared at me and my peculiar arm, writing notes whilst the consultant spoke.

"What are the blood results?" Dr Lu murmured.

"We are just waiting on them. They should be here by noon," the small, older, head consultant murmured.

"How could this have happened? Her pulse is still racing. What on earth happened?'" Dr Lu demanded.

"We just don't know. If it's what we were thinking, I mean, the symptoms do suggest. . ." the head consultant trailed off helplessly.

"I daren't think," Dr Lu groaned nervously, before gazing one last time at the beeping monitor before she left the room.

Amidst my confusion and fear over what I had overheard, Mum arrived. Everything was going to be alright now she was here, even if she was only allowed to wash me.

The door swung open and Dr Lu came hurrying in, out of breath from her race to get to me.

"It must be stopped!" She gathered her breath. "She has toxic levels of amitriptyline in her blood. I mean her heart, what damage it must be doing, I cannot imagine!"

Mum gaped at this nutty doctor in disbelief.

"She will have to be taken off the drug immediately; there's no time to let her come off it slowly. She can never have it again. She's allergic; it doesn't metabolise in her blood."

You can safely say that 'she' was taken off the drug with immediate effect. Amitriptyline can cause long term detrimental effects on the liver and heart, which can often be fatal. One could say I'd had yet another lucky escape.

Welcome
To The
Promised Land

CHAPTER TWELVE

The One-Way Ticket to the Promised Land

Finally, after my parents had endured many conversations with the Primary Care Trust, we were going to be on our way to The Promised Land. I had waited half a year for this moment.

It was with a small pang of regret, alongside anticipation, that I left my homely Sunshine Ward. Leaving behind the place that had grown so accustomed to my presence.

As my room had slowly been dismantled—the posters covering the walls taken down and the teddies from all of my friends packed up—it had reverted back into nothing more than a plain hospital room. The windows with their blinds that felt like my prison wardens for so long, now seemed to be waving me off with friendly affirmation.

I wasn't scared of going to The Promised Land because they were going to fix me there: it had said that in the brochure Mum had read out.

If it was the place that would rid me of the chronic exhaustion that plagued my every moment like a swarm of hornets around my head seeping poison into my veins, then it was worth going for. The brochure said they could manage the fatigue and the unbearable pain, so I had no doubt they would do it.

I only have flickers of what happened on the journey to The Promised Land: the whispers of good luck in my ears as the paramedics took my weakened body on the trolley through the endless corridors of bright flashes of lights with a blanket covering my face.

I was hauled inside the ambulance by two gifted paramedics who accompanied Dad, who, of course, was well trained at this job. Mum followed in the car behind, carrying all my possessions with her.

The cool, outside air graced my nostrils, travelled deep into my lungs. It was so incredibly fresh that it lifted my spirits even more—if that was at all possible. But I hadn't readied myself for the thunderous noise of the ambulance.

The engine roared with delight and the back shook like a mini earthquake. The intense sensory overload was too much for me to handle; the pain throbbed inside. There was light, there was noise, it was already too much for my senses and we had yet to even begin. I groaned to exclaim my discomfort but the ambulance wouldn't listen!

Dad, who was sitting next to me and chatting quietly to his old crew mate, quickly put an oxygen mask over my face.

"Breathe into this sweetheart, it will make it easier," he kindly offered, before the ambulance simultaneously grumbled and started to move. I was off!

I flinched with every road noise, the sounds penetrating the silence amongst the passengers in the back of the van. As I began to breathe in the mixture of oxygen and nitrous oxide, there to fog my sensations, my body started to tingle. The noise became less of a crash and more of a gentle push. The sound assault filled my head and temporarily made me forget all my thoughts as my senses continued to go into overload. I felt more and more detached from the body that was crippling up in pain until there was nothing. Limbo Land took over.

I could hear Dad's murmurs. Through my dark glasses, I could see that he was standing, looking at me, with a worried expression in his eyes.

"Nearly there, honey."

The ambulance jolted to a stop.

The trolley was lifted off the vehicle and we began the ride through the hospital to find out where to go. Everything was new and had a clinical feel to it. Once we arrived at our destination, called Desert Ward, there was suddenly a piercing sound—a fire siren—and the doors slammed shut. It was excruciatingly loud.

I groaned to try and drown out the sound. A traumatic welcome to The Promised Land and one that would be repeated weekly thanks to the regular fire alarms tests.

I'm here though, I thought. *In the place people talk about, where miracles can happen.*

That was the image they liked to portray. If only it were true, but I wasn't to know. There was barely any space for belongings: just a drawer in the single bedside unit. Everything about this place was loud and bright to me, despite what the booklet had promised.

There was a note on the table from one of the other patients. Her name was Belle. She introduced herself and sent her love, hoping we could meet to talk. At this point, she was also bedridden but could talk and move for herself.

Another lady, who was next to me, used a hair dryer and could walk around by herself. This gave me hope, even if the hairdryer drove me crazy.

For the first time, I was seeing people of all different spectrums of M.E. all in one place.

A male Asian nurse came in to introduce himself.

'Hi, my name is Clive. I am the CFS nurse.' He was quiet and handsome with big brown eyes but not very tall.

A sudden heavy click-clack, click-clack of heels built towards a crescendo, until my ears felt like they would explode from the stabbing sound.

Please stop, I helplessly prayed. *Please God, make it stop.*

I hadn't even thought that there would be a person accompanying the sound because it had entered my brain as nothing more than noise, painful noise. It eventually stopped, but not until after the damage had been done to my throbbing head.

"Hi, I will be Jessica's Occupational Health Therapist," a foreign voice said coolly.

I wondered what nationality she was because I recognised the accent, but before I could decide the conversation had continued on without me.

"I see," Mum acknowledged. "Well, considering you work with noise-sensitive patients, I would have thought you would have worn more suitable shoes."

I opened my screwed-up eyes briefly to note a middle-aged lady with blonde straw-like hair that reminded me of a scarecrow. The word certainly did seem to fit her persona but I felt wrong labelling her like this.

I imagined a cartoon of her and Mum coming to blows. She just didn't look like a woman who would listen, let alone back down. I was right.

"She is to be subjected to more noise and light. This is part of the programme here, so she will get accustomed to it," she replied arrogantly.

Before fading out, I decided that the name Scarecrow would definitely be sticking.

"Jess can't even press the buzzer; surely a side room, where it's quieter, would be more appropriate for her? Instead of this bay," was the next thing I heard Mum say.

"We don't normally supply a side room. I shall see if there is one, but I very much doubt it."

I will never know for a fact but I could bet you a million dollars that the newly christened Scarecrow did not go to the effort of seeing if there was one; it just didn't seem to be her style.

The exhaustion, the pain, the suffering, the light, the noise—all jumbled up into Limbo Land this time. Once again, I felt that I was swaying onboard a boat at sea in a storm. The sounds poured into my dream-state and my heart pummelled inside my chest, whilst sweat poured down my freezing cold body.

I groaned, trying to make sense of this version of events, but I couldn't think through the never-ending noise. Tears started to fall slowly down my face. This wasn't what The Promised Land had promised in the brochure! Surely this was only a bad dream, a misunderstanding.

It is going to go quiet in a moment, I told myself.

Mum held me tightly with a hug that cured everything. It was okay, my mum was here. She would stand up for me. She would be my voice. I needed somebody there who I could talk to, someone who would understand my clicking sounds and mumbled whispers, and piece them together into a sentence.

So, the next piece of information came as quite a shock: no visitors until the weekend. Mum held me tightly to her, as a lump filled my throat.

Please don't go, I thought.

I didn't know a life on my own, a life without somebody friendly close by that I knew. What was I going to do?

I pictured her smile; I imagined her warm arms around me whilst I listened to her and Dad being forced to leave me. I had no idea what was going to happen next, but one thing was for sure: I was going to be on my own in this place.

If all this trauma was part of the programme that was going to make me better, then I would go along with it. Was this what would make me get better? Having huge amounts of noise and bright lights in my every moment? I was sceptical, but I wanted to believe.

*

I was now facing the world alone with the constant light and sound torturing my very existence. I was holding on though, grimly frozen on the path they had set me on, like a rabbit in the headlights.

The nurses seemed nice enough and Clive nursed me for

the first few weeks day in and day out. He attended to all my needs, as I was not fit to do anything for myself—including not being able to get help when I needed it.

I was in a strange place, without anyone I knew, with no friends or family, for the first time in my life, and I loathed every second of it.

CHAPTER THIRTEEN

Lost for Words

The days were long, followed by stressful nights, yet there was no real change physically. I had been expecting big differences but this seemed to just be another hospital that was louder. Sounds came at me from all directions.

I was petrified, now I was on my own with no real contact with my family. As I was not practising my newly found code or my movements, they seemed to be lost. Bug had been vital in changing how isolating life had been for the past six months.

What could I do to nurse my poor, throbbing head? The exhaustion was such that I could barely lift an eyelid. The journey to get to The Promised Land had wrecked me but, as I had proven on multiple occasions, I was not easily beaten.

I took myself back to Scotland, back to the fresh open air and back to quad biking across the Scottish valleys with Dad. Here, the sound of my quad bike's motor was the only noise in the otherwise blissful silence. We followed hills and pathways into the forest, mountains either side of us, until we reached a river. The water cascaded over our bikes, but we just revved our engines and were gone into the distance.

Wild deer raced away through the bracken and, overhead, the sweet sound of a golden eagle blessed the day. Laughter and joy spread across my face as together we took on the world. My reverie came to a sudden halt with the crash of the medication trolley.

A doctor came in; she was American or Australian. My brain wasn't registering the sounds properly. She listened to my heart as it pummelled heavily in my chest.

"We shall get a scan of that. Got to get you well, kiddo!" she said encouragingly.

This sounded positive. Maybe *this* was the doctor who was going to get me better. Maybe now I was in the proper hospital for M.E. and things would change.

"Do you have problems sleeping, Jess?"

I tried to nod and my neck jerked. It must have looked like a slight shake of my head, for the answer was not the one I had hoped to hear.

"Ah well, I'm glad to hear it."

No! No! No! I yelled but the words did not form. Frustratingly, since the journey, I had lost all that I had gained in previous months. Plus, no one apart from my parents understood my code.

That is not what I meant! Please come back. No, really! I need your help, I desperately thought as I watched her walk out of my cubicle, oblivious to my insistent, disillusioned groans.

The energy fast deserted me. My heart started to race and my head was burning. I tried to reach the surface, but Limbo Land sucked all the strength out of my breath and I was gone.

I awoke to searing agony pulsing through my body. I was

stuck on my side. Half of my body had gone painfully numb from the weight of the rest of my body. If only I could call for some much-needed help, if I could just bloody move! But nobody was there to listen to my tiny yelps of pain.

Frustration at my incapacity, frustration at this life of mine, flooded through me as I lay there, incapable of reaching anybody.

Exhausted by my efforts, I tried to zone out of the pain and make it separate from my body. Even in a busy hospital, noisy with the sound of people and machines, it was incredible how the loneliness could make you feel as if there was nobody there.

Finally, there was the soft sound of footsteps. *Thank God, surely this would be someone to help.* Despite the sheer exhaustion from my efforts, I groaned one last time.

"Hmmm... H-h-e-l-p... Hmmm!"

The code that would be perfectly understood by my parents was hit-or-miss here.

I couldn't even see outside of my cubicle; the light blinding me to the extent that I couldn't bear to have the curtains opened to see the rest of the four bedded bay I was in. This left me alone, all on my own, as I couldn't even press the buzzer to ask for help.

"Hmmm!" My hope of being heard was disappearing fast.

Then someone popped their head around the curtain and utter relief surged through me. Not for long, I hasten to add. It was a psychologist who found the noises interesting, rather than recognising them as a cry for help.

"You must be in a lot of pain," she said slowly, extending each syllable of the phrase.

I don't need pity, I need help! I thought desperately. *Could she not see the discomfort?*

"I wonder what got you here. You are new aren't you?" she said in the same patronising voice.

Geez, this was slow torture!

"H-h-h-elp!" I stammered in despair.

She seemed to understand that something wasn't right and left the cubicle at last.

Scarecrow's click-clacking heels came into the foreground and she arrived with a physiotherapist. Even though compassion was not her greatest asset, my priority was to get moved quickly.

"Ahh. . . ha. . . ahh," was the only sound I could make.

"You need to tell us what's wrong, Jess," she said with harsh authority.

It was going to be a long, hard day. There would be no audible words for Scarecrow, as she was not taking the time to listen to my code that had worked perfectly well on Sunshine ward.

*

Scarecrow was a formidable character. In her opinion she was beyond compare to anyone else. It was her way, or the highway, and the highway became ever more inviting, the more she visited me.

From what I had gathered of this strange setup, an Occupational Health Therapist (Scarecrow), alongside a physiotherapist, were assigned to each of the eight resident M.E. sufferers. There were two bays with four people in each.

Renowned for their extreme pacing regime of rest and

activity, The Promised Land used a mixture of graded exercise therapy (known as GET) and cognitive behavioural therapy (known as CBT). There were no other treatment options available on the National Health Service, according to the research my parents had done.

Boss Man, the specialist, came to visit every month or two but otherwise it was left to the M.E. team to access every situation. However, Boss Man made the final decisions.

BANG! CRASH!

My head jerked and winced with every sound. Somebody in the corner was being moved on a transfer. I tried, I really did, to block the noise out and listen to what Scarecrow was saying to me. I had gone from a room where noise was made minimal to a different universe. My brain was over-stimulated. With tears in my eyes, I tried to plough through the noise and concentrate on her voice.

"Look at me, Jessica. You need to calm down," she said assertively.

I felt like I was being beaten black and blue by the sound alone.

"Look at me, Jess. We really need to do something about your—"

Please goddamn, stop the explosion of sound, please.

I pleaded with the noise being made by the ambulance crew. How was I going to cope with this? Torturous sound all around me—I felt every crash go through me, along with the booming voices reverberating around my head. I needed to take myself away, use my mind to distract from the aural assault, but I couldn't master myself; I was trapped in the moment.

What was this place? Why was everything so horrendously

loud? I refused to figuratively hold up the white flag; I wouldn't surrender to this pain. If only I could just hold my burning head, but my arms did not move so that respite was out of the question.

I had not seen a physiotherapist every day so my limbs were stiffening greatly. Then, as a warrior does, I metaphorically flung my arms up and made ready for one more battle to conquer the escalating situation.

I imagined that the noises were the soundtrack for my favourite piece of classical music: an orchestral piece used in *The Lord of the Rings* victory fight. The chatter became the sound of orchestral violins; the machines became the rhythm; and Scarecrow's voice was the treble of the choir boys singing. I mentally played the other instruments to try and manage the sound.

"You need to concentrate!" Scarecrow barked.

Did she not know the battle I was fighting? The battle that I had found a way to win. I was conducting the noise instead of allowing it to consume me. If it were a case of just concentrating, I would have done that at the beginning.

Then I crashed into Limbo Land. Sound mixed with light, my heart started to race, a cold sweat streamed down me, my eyes throbbed with the light and I was gone.

*

I had made it to Friday when the specialist doctor came to visit. I called it Judgment Day. This is when all the medical staff come around in a group, headed by the doctor, to assess my situation.

When it had just been the American doctor (whom I named Boss Man's sidekick) visiting, she had been respectful of my noise sensitivity. Instead of her voice, I could hear a male voice, that got louder when he entered the room, accompanied by the patter of footsteps outside my cubicle curtain.

Even with dark glasses on, the room was too bright for me. I understood that I would need to tackle this but surely if they treated my symptoms first then it would get easier? I thought it was going to be about making me better, not hurting me.

At first, they had been lenient about allowing the curtains to stay drawn but this man was brash. He ruthlessly started pulling back the curtains, letting in the bright light.

"She will never get better if she doesn't try! Light sensitivity is the first thing we need to deal with, you know that," he said loudly so everybody could hear.

The words stung me; he knew nothing of my plight!

He arrived in my room, which had been decorated with pictures of Becky, Tom and the rest of my family, alongside the beautiful images of Scotland and Bluebell Hill that Dad had put up with all the cards.

He looked at me, surrounded by his crowd of followers. There was a change in the atmosphere with his arrival: everything suddenly became very prim and proper.

Once they had all gathered, I was able to see him. He looked rather like an old headmaster of mine. The short, slightly rotund figure peered at me.

"What have we here? You must get better. The light stays and those glasses will be off, I will be looking at those arms too. Work hard in physio, get them moving—you can't have them not straightening like that," he barked with authority. "Are you here to get better?"

Yes Sir!

"He's the boss man. What he says goes!" chirped the friendly American doctor, Boss Man's Sidekick, easing the tense atmosphere somewhat.

So, this was the Boss Man who had been talked about so much. This was the specialist doctor whom I had come to be treated by.

My arms were generally bent so tightly that my finger would reach my ear. I was scared of having them moved away from me because then I would have to come to terms with not having my ear plugs in fully. I used the only movement I had in my body to push them back in for the noise was unbearable.

As he did his rounds, he reached Belle in the corner. The discussion with the other doctors became more and more heated, until he shouted.

"You will not get into Oxford or Cambridge like this. You do NOT have chronic fatigue syndrome; you have an eating disorder!"

The room was stunned; my heart hammered. I shook for her. Belle was the kindest soul, who had really tried to help me by sending messages via nurses. To have her most intimate problem broadcast like that seemed cruel and inappropriate. I could hear her crying. No one spoke up or comforted her. They just trooped out of the cubicle as if nothing had happened.

The occupational health therapists came round afterwards

to see us individually and check that we were okay. But I was mortified to see that nobody went into Belle's cubicle even though we could all hear her tears.

*

Nicky was next door to me and Karen was opposite, whilst Belle was diagonal to me. Despite not knowing what each other even looked like at the beginning, there was a fast-growing, strong connection between all the girls in bay four and we were able to communicate via coding.

We didn't ever venture out of our cubicles due to the disease, yet not only were we roomies—we were each other's support in the week.

Girls, what is your favourite colour? As you know I think pink, I love pink and anything with the slightest bit of Disney in it. Tell me all about you!

Love Belle x

When my family and Nick came to visit at the weekend, I would write back through coding. My lovely friend Nick was becoming quite good at coding too, and even though I only saw him every fortnight just for a few minutes, it felt like a blessed relief to see someone from the outside world.

Hey Belle,

Fave colour is blue but I love Pirates of the Caribbean! Me in a sandwich between Orlando Bloom and Johnny Depp sounds like a good idea, don't you think? I hated the way Boss

Man spoke to you. I'm sorry, he was awful. If I could speak, I would have stuck up for you. Makes me so angry.

Love Jess x

Hey Belle and Jess,

Just got your messages, what a perfect sandwich! I'm a Christian and I believe that one day I will be able to help kids who got ill at a young age like me with M.E. It has been a long time, this place is my last hope.

Love Nicky x

Hi Nicky, Jess and Belle,

I have been ill for some time, my worst symptom is the exhaustion. I mean sheer exhaustion. I washed my face on my own for the first time in years. You know how damn good that feels? Those nurses miss the really important bits like behind your ears! You know all about that, don't you Jess?

Love Karen x

Dear Karen,

Yes! I know exactly what you mean. Oh how I long for the day to touch my face and be able to pick a spot. I wouldn't mind looking like Rudolph the Red Nosed Reindeer if that meant I had got rid of the yuck inside the blasted thing!

Love Jess x

Dear Jess, Karen and Nicky,

Tell me a bit about how it started for you. How did you get ill? I was just about to do my A-Levels and then it all went wrong. I want to be a doctor so badly, but now I don't know whether that will happen. I've been bedbound for a year. I feel too exhausted to be able to get out and hold my weight but I can move around the bed.

Love Belle x

Dear Belle, Jess and Nicky,

Before I was ill, I used to travel the world and see the seven wonders—the world was my oyster. I was an archaeologist. I got a virus and got sick. I'd been waiting years to get into this place. Boss Man thought I'd actually been suffering for many years previously but it took over my thirties. At least I had travelled somewhere. I'm getting some of my independence back and can't wait to sit on the actual toilet! Instead of all these stupid bedpans and commodes—there is nothing like the real thing.

Love Karen x

Dear Belle, Nicky and Karen,

I got ill after a flu virus, it happened quickly in reality, yet it felt a long time too. After leaving school, six months later I was in hospital and I have been there ever since. Sorry, can't code anymore—brain hurting.

Love Jess x

Dear Jess, Belle and Karen,

Sorry you are suffering quite so much Jess, we are praying for you. There must be a plan somewhere. I'm learning to stand again. It will start with only weight bearing, which is amazing, and then I will start taking a few steps. My aim is five steps to the bathroom. You won't know this Jess, but there is a bathroom next door to me. There is one in each bay, I'm told. What is your worse symptom? Mine is the crippling exhaustion, I hate it.

Love Nicky x

Dear Nicky, Belle and Karen,

Oh, the eye pain is chronic from all this light. I can't quite believe why they have to have it so bright in these rooms. They are going to be taking away my dark glasses soon and I'm so scared. I find it hard to see even with them on. Can you give me any advice?

Love Jess x

Dear Jess,

It does get easier, I promise. My heart goes out to you, it really does. It is horrible to start with. Hopefully, they will do it slowly and not suddenly. Don't be scared, we shall all support you, like you did for me.

In understanding, Belle x

Dear Belle,

Thank you, I can't help but feel very overwhelmed. I'm trying everything but I can't seem to break away from this cocoon. I want to be the butterfly, not the caterpillar stuck inside. When I was in Sunshine Ward, I had a room and whilst I didn't have you three, I had my family. My mum is a nurse and my dad is a paramedic so they would be able to tell me what the hell is going on here. The doctors don't even talk to me. They just prescribe things. I'm still a person, not just a bed number. I can't wait to one day meet you.

Love Jess x

Dear Belle, Nicky and Karen,

What's your wildest story of misunderstanding? Mine was some nutty psychologist, who I nicknamed Psycho Woman. She was a nightmare. Always trying to lock me up in some psychiatric unit. She didn't understand a sense of humour if it smacked her in the face. The joy came when she actually took the time to read my coded diary. It was only then that she believed I was not suffering from depression.

Love Jess x

Dear Jess,

Just yesterday, I was taken for a scan and the person doing it said, "Oh you've got M.E.? All you need is a bottle of Lucozade and a go on the treadmill love." I know, shocking! I told her she had no understanding of M.E. but in the end I found myself laughing at her for being so ignorant. Thank God for a sense of humour!

Love Nicky x

Dear Jess and Nicky,

Oh, it is such a shame that we have to have shocker tales about how they perceive our own health. But yes, similar stories of being told to liven up and start dancing are a few that make me wince or cry with laughter, dependent on the day.

Love Karen

Dear Jess, Nicky and Karen,

I have too many stories to start listing them but a lot of them happened here actually. It's amazing what happens when you have no way of standing up to people.

Love Belle x

Over the next few months, all three of the girls started to make improvements. It was with a tinge of sadness, I watched as each of the girls started to grow stronger, but I didn't start to improve. In fact, my arms were becoming stiffer and could not move even with help.

The physiotherapist would try to move them passively, yet they could only straighten to an angle of ten percent. All these changes were concerning. I was so proud of each of them, but I felt like my body was failing me.

Each of us had a deep understanding of a chunk of what the others were going through because we were all there for the long haul. I was no longer the newbie so the other girls were used to my difficulties.

Dear Belle,

I hear you stood up for the first time today—that's amazing! Well done! Just a short message to say you are fabulous. I'm blessed to know you. Got to go, I'm exhausted but just wanted to congratulate you!

Love Jess x

Dear Jess,

Thank you, it will happen for you too. I'm sure of it. I've got some news for you—we've got a surprise for you! Finally, we shall see each other face to face. Can all four of us play a little game tonight? I'm giving you the questions and you need to answer them, then we will guess who is who.

Love Belle x

At exactly eight in the evening, Karen made her way from

opposite me to sit next to me. It was astonishing to see her face not far from mine, for her to be touching my hand, after all this time. It had now been three months since Karen had arrived. She was up and walking a few stumbled steps.

After that, Nicky came through the curtain to my left, and I saw her for the first time. I had never seen her face before, and it was even prettier than I had imagined it, with a huge smile that was incredibly special.

Lastly, Belle joined this momentous occasion. I was so happy and emotional that they had all gone to so much effort to help me join in. We played 'Who said what?' where we had to guess everyone's answers.

It was so much fun but soon enough Limbo Land snapped me out of our fun and my body shook with uncontrollable tremors.

Hey Jess, Nicky and Karen,

It was so lovely to see you last night. Your kindness to me will be remembered. I have enjoyed spending time with you and our little chats, through all the notes. I've nearly run out of notepads!

It's been great getting to know you but it is time for me to say goodbye. My funding to stay here has run out, and I'm looking forward to being with my family, as I'm sure you can imagine.

This means new things though for the unit. Jess, you have now taken my title of 'ME Granny.' You are now the oldest but youngest person on this ward. Let me explain—you have been on this ward for the longest amount of time now, making you a granny! We arrange for the little gifts to be bought for those who are leaving. I know you will do a fab job. Here are my details and we will keep in touch.

Love Belle x

Many months after Belle had left the unit, it was discovered that she did not have an eating disorder. She sent me a card confirming she actually had an undiagnosed form of lupus.

I had been so angry at the injustice of this and how she was treated. It didn't make me feel particularly confident with the doctors but it took her many months to tell me that a blood test done by her doctor at home had shown this. She was too frightened to ever stand up to Boss Man.

CHAPTER FOURTEEN

Straighteners

Boss Man came marching in with a bigger crowd than usual. They were talking in deep, hushed voices about the latest news on Parkinson's disease. This doctor, with his stout figure, was an impressive force in the medical world, or so it seemed.

I had grown used to Judgement Day by then, when Boss Man would cast his opinion upon me. You didn't mess with Boss Man.

"Ah now, let me see," he mused. "This is our very special patient. She has a very rare form of fatigue syndrome. It's a life-threatening condition. You see here—"

He pointed to my limp arms that were folded up by my ears.

"This is contraction. She came to us like that. If she was well enough, she would be having an operation to straighten them. Arms must be able to straighten and bend, otherwise this happens."

He swung a hand at my arms. "If you don't move the arms, you will lose the ability to move them for the long term. The tendons shorten and that means trouble."

The students gawped and hurriedly took notes. It was if he were a salesman and I was the object on sale. The constant stares always made me feel uncomfortable; that and his oscillating temper made Judgement Day even more difficult. But I knew that I hadn't come to him with contraction of my arms. I was sure of it.

A meeting was scheduled between him and my parents—if only I could be a fly on the wall for that one. Mum and Dad arrived in my cubicle in the middle of Judgement Day, both trying to envisage what the 'great man' would look like, as they hadn't met him before.

He was something of a legend. Apparently 'one of the only doctors in the UK to take M.E. seriously.' But they were about to meet the real man behind the legend.

*

My parents came into my cubicle after the meeting, looking haggard and, much later, described to me exactly what had happened. They both sat nervously chatting with one another in the meeting room waiting for Boss Man to come in.

Boss Man had an aura surrounding him, one that didn't bear messing with. Yet, so too did my dad, who was a tall, kind version of Boss Man. Dad was recognised for making his point known and it would be no different today. Nobody scared him.

Dad said Boss Man's entrance broke their conversation and it was not long before he was in full flow of being the centre of attention.

"She has a 20% chance of dying from this," he revealed.

This punctured the atmosphere somewhat and raised a current of confusion and fear.

"Right, I see." Dad held onto his nerve.

"She is a very poorly young lady. I'm sure you know," Boss

Man continued. "So, I just want you to know where we stand. Her arms are our next problem. Really, she needs to have an operation to straighten them."

"Okay," Dad said assertively. "Isn't it strange how this has happened?"

"It is regrettable that it was left to happen at her last hospital—" Boss Man began, before Dad interrupted him.

"But she was responding to passive movements. Her limbs were more pliable and we could get her arm down to her tummy quite easily," he said coolly.

Suddenly, the air was whipped into a storm of anger and Boss Man started to rage.

"Your daughter did NOT deteriorate under my care!"

"I wasn't suggesting that she had deteriorated, I merely wanted to ask you why Jess's arms had contracted—" Dad began calmly.

This was the limit. Boss Man didn't want the truth being spoken. For someone to suggest that a patient had slightly deteriorated under his care was an absolute outrage and he would not stand for it.

"LET ME MAKE THIS QUITE CLEAR. YOUR DAUGHTER HAS NOT DETERIORATED UNDER MY CARE!"

Getting louder and louder with every word he spat out, surely nobody would dare to disagree with him! However, he had not previously come up against my dad, who had moved heaven and earth to get me to this place and would quite rightly speak his mind. The love for a child is a bond of far greater power than anything Boss Man had in his arsenal. Boss Man did not take kindly to this challenge.

*

A little later in the day, my eyes opened to a great sea of people huddled around my bed talking loudly to one another. There was one man heading this conversation; he was a tall, well-dressed Asian doctor wearing a Simpsons tie. He turned his attention to me.

"Can you move your arms at all, Jess?" he asked, imitating the motion.

Why do all the doctors assume that, because I can't speak, I must be stupid? I wondered, as I slightly shook my head.

"No?"

That was generally what a shake meant, but do I nod or shake now? This was important information! If I nodded, then was I agreeing to the answer being no or by shaking my head, was I affirming my original answer again? I decided to opt with the latter and shook my head.

Before I knew it, the day of the operation to straighten my arms had arrived. I had been told that it would consist of putting me to sleep and forcing my arms to straighten. Whilst under anaesthetic, my body shouldn't feel pain so they will be able to straighten it unlike when I'm awake because the excruciating discomfort is too much to bear.

My arms had been assessed and they were now in a terrible state. It had been eight months of not having regular passive movements through the day that had made this a real problem.

Previously on Sunshine Ward, I had my parents there, which meant I didn't need my arms bent.

I was scared because although I had been put to sleep before, I didn't want to imagine the other side, but before I knew it

I was travelling the length of the hospital to the operating theatre, with Dad by my side.

Moments later, I was breathing in oxygen whilst other drugs were put into me. As Dad held onto my hand, I floated into a distant dream-like world, far away from the pain and suffering.

*

I awoke to an excruciating agony. Groaning was the only external sign I could give but inside I was screaming with the pain forcing its way up and down my arms.

I was disorientated and lost—trapped in the torment of exceeding the upper limits a pain scale could reach. I breathed heavily as the oxygen mask drowned out my groans.

Screaming.

I didn't know how long I could keep this up; it was as if my body was on a torturous stretching rack.

Shit! Where are my hands?

I looked down and saw the huge casts on each arm.

Screaming.

Bloody hell, where is everybody? For a moment, I thought I had awoken mid-operation. *Pain. Where's my dad?*

A nurse came rushing to my aid, yet she could not help the pain. She could barely understand me.

Screaming.

Dad appeared and he tried to understand my whimpers. The agony was like being hanged by my arms, stretching and stretching, nothing to help them.

Screaming.

I whimpered my way through the night. Thick, heavy

exhaustion hit me head-on again and again and again. It was like I was stuck on replay.

When morning came, I wanted the consultant to explain why I was in so much pain, but he didn't. He looked at his stunning work with a huge sense of pride, paying no mind to the agony he had caused.

From what I could gather there was some problem with my left arm. What it was I did not know. To my horror, they brought in an electric saw.

"Alright Jess, we need to cut away a square in the middle of the cast. This is the only way we can do it."

I couldn't even nod my head for the shock was like being hit with a brick. The physiotherapist I called 'Tall' helped Clive to look after me but they could do nothing to defend me against the noise. It seemed amplified and felt a thousand times louder than anything I had ever heard before. I felt as if my head would explode. The pounding in my head lasted way longer than the actual sawing.

Once the square had been cut and removed, a sharp sting erupted out of nowhere to reveal an open sore on the inner crease of my elbow. It needed cleaning and dressing by Clive. It stung like a bitch.

The pain of the operation in conjunction with the open skin wound lasted weeks. The operation had mainly been a success. The surgeon had attempted to fully straighten my arms from the contracture but my left tendon had already shortened slightly.

My pain relief had been upped due to the feeble moans of agony I could just about muster to show how much pain I was in.

CHAPTER FIFTEEN

Potions Class

It was November and not long after the operation to straighten both of my arms had been completed. I was still in agony, and although my arms were mostly straight in huge casts, it proved difficult to manage the pain levels.

The drug round was a bit like a potions class in a *Harry Potter* book. I would watch the nurses put together all the bright colours of the different medications throughout the day that were prescribed to help my body. On top of these potions, I also had morphine patches.

The doctors added different medications without actually telling me what they were for. Not being able to talk and ask questions was so frustrating. It would have been so much easier if my parents could have been there to do it for me. The list of drugs I was on had become unbearably long since the operation.

I lay there, looking like a cartoon character, with my arms in big casts on both sides, but the reality was that I was riddled with pain and unable to scratch that itch on the side of my nose.

I still couldn't get used to my parents not being there. I needed somebody to listen to my needs or to simply give me a drink. I wanted somebody to take in the information from the ward round and to then explain it to me. Instead, there would be more bottles of medication and no explanation from anyone.

The potions class started in the morning. There were different measuring pots and syringes of all shapes and sizes. As was once said to me, it would be a junkie's heaven (please note the dry sense of humour)!

First, they would flush water down my NG tube, which made me feel unwell. The medication would go down next but sometimes they pushed it too hard and my tummy would gurgle. I was a mine of information on NG tubes. Whenever they were teaching a student, I always felt like I could have quite happily joined in with the instructing.

After the medication had been administered it was usually just a waiting game. We had to wait for the meds to kick in and then wait for the next part of my schedule to come around.

But on one particular day I got really dizzy, my eyes felt like they belonged to someone else, and then I was sick.

Fortunately, thanks to great dedication to finding a way for me to use my blasted buzzer myself, my two physiotherapists, Tiny and Tall, along with Scarecrow, had realised if the buzzer was positioned on my chin, the slight movement of my head would press the extra sensitive button.

It had taken over a year to work this out, and for me to have the stamina to move my head far enough. What a relief it was, especially now.

I buzzed for some help just before I was sick again. By the time the student nurse arrived, I was coming to the spectacular grand finale. I threw up the entire contents of my stomach around my NG tube. The vomit was going up my nose as well as out of my mouth.

She panicked and shouted for help whilst I gagged and groaned. The tube was thankfully pulled out in the end and I was cleaned up, restoring me with some sort of dignity.

I was now ready for a new tube to be passed but sadly I was sick again, the M.E. Monster was showing no mercy.

They managed, after many attempts, to get the tube down but I was continuously sick throughout the procedure. I went from having my myriad of potions to nothing at all.

After more than one day of this, I started to feel the unbearable pain that the medication had been suppressing. The pain made my body shake uncontrollably but I was still sick whenever any food was brought near me.

My bed and I went on numerous adventures to have different tests in the bid to find something that could be treated. I had an ultrasound and a CT scan. There was even a test in which they took lots of X-rays, whilst a special liquid was fed down the NG tube. This was to see if there was a blockage in my small intestine, but nothing showed up.

The withdrawal symptoms from having no medication at all (even the morphine patches had been taken off) were extreme and worsened by the day. Cold sweats started to run down me; my legs were shaking and felt as if ants were scurrying up and down them.

This pain was different to that of an ordinary achy sore. I couldn't keep still without yelping and groaning as the agony took over. Then it reached my back and, before long, it took over my whole body.

Normally, night-time is for sleeping but my nights were

spent constantly pressing the buzzer for the nurse. My bed was left quite high because, normally, I couldn't move but the situation was totally different when I was in a shaking cold sweat. I couldn't lie on just one side for long without my whole body shaking.

My veins were usually a nightmare to get a needle into, however they had managed to find one vein which had taken a cannula. It was precious and was the only means for me to get any kind of intravenous pain relief.

One night, I had been positioned on my left side, my arms were still in big casts and I was a little too close to the edge of the bed. It only took one violent shake and the worst happened: I felt myself begin to fall out of the bed.

I tried to stop with all my might but I was helpless in a broken body and I continued to fall in a bizarre slow motion before my head crashed onto the floor and I lay in a heap on the cold, hard surface, barely able to breathe due to the shooting pain.

It took a hoist to get me back onto the bed, as they aren't allowed to pick you up in case they injure themselves. It took all night for me to recover the smallest bit, as my head ached from the bang. Before dawn, an investigation into how my fall could have happened was underway.

Nobody knew what to do to help. I was in visible agony, still shaking. They couldn't get the drugs that would help me down my NG tube without me bringing them back up and the cannula had been lost in my fall out of bed so they had to resort to injections.

The injections gave me thirty minutes' relief but I could only have them once every four hours. I passed the minutes by counting and watching the big clock. It was my only means of survival.

See if you can make it to twenty, I desperately told myself.

1, 2, 3, 4, 5, 6, 7, 8, 9, 10. . .

I desperately wanted my mum, my dad, my brother, my sister, and my grandparents. Who are the people you turn to when everything goes wrong? In my case, it was my family.

. . . 11, 12, 13, 14, 15, 16, 17, 18, 19, 20 . . .

I was just sixteen and, at this moment I was living for the next injection. The only thing available to ease some of my suffering. Never did I contemplate that this would be the rest of my life. Then again, I had never imagined that I would be bedridden, unable to move and completely dependent on others.

Just keep holding on for another second, I continuously told myself.

. . . 21, 22, 23, 24, 25, 26, 27, 28, 29, 30. . .

Mum sat by my side throughout visiting times. She sat very still and read to me from a magazine or the latest *Harry Potter* book. Not that I could concentrate on the words. Mum's voice was enough to give me something to try and hold on to.

Becky would sit there quietly, deep in thought, but her simple presence was enough of a comfort.

I was only vaguely able to remember when Nick visited but I had no recollection of what he was trying to say because the pain took over every inch of my body and memory. This did not stop him from religiously visiting me and trying to calm my agony. It was a comfort to feel his presence, despite what I was going through.

Boss Man's sidekick had even been called in on her day off

in the first week of my new symptoms but there was nothing she could do without being able to get something into that NG tube.

. . . 31, 32, 33, 34, 35, 36, 37, 38, 39, 40. . .

Gran and Pop came to visit with a surprise from my cousins: a beautifully drawn, massive, cut-out mural, decorated with delicate artwork and sparkle. Gran held onto my hand, she had always been so good at that, and whispered encouragements.

"You are just lovely,' she said. "So lovely. Do you remember our book? We are going to write that book together. One day we will tell the world your story and we will write it together."

. . . 41, 42, 43. 44, 45, 46, 47, 48, 49, 50 . . .

Of course I remembered. I remembered her delicate hands holding mine, as she promised me that we would write that story together. That had been a year ago.

I had always enjoyed reading and writing, and had excelled at English at school. I loved the concept of creating lives and being able to tell precious stories, allowing others into my imagination so that my stories could become special to them too, simply by the words that I used. It is somewhat magical, don't you think?

"Go back to Bluebell Hill, Jess. One day we shall walk there together," Pop softly whispered, so only Gran and I could hear. She nodded enthusiastically, willing me to rest.

Bluebell Hill, I thought as my body finally rested for a few moments.

After a while, drugs were slowly introduced into my system via the NG tube. Any pain relief was warmly welcomed by my exhausted body. It needed all the help it could get. This saga went on for three weeks and, throughout this time, I had blood tests taken most days. After several attempts on my feet and hands, they usually ended up drawing the blood from my groin as my arms were still hidden, now in braces instead of casts.

Having bloods taken from your groin is about as horrific as it sounds! It is essential that you stay completely still (hardly a problem in my case!) but it just feels so unnatural to have needles going into that area.

In the short time that I had been in casts, my arms had become completely stiff and rigid. The hope had been that my arms would remain straight but, as usual, my body had its own plan. When my arms were freed from the casts, they began the excruciating process of trying to contract back up to my biceps again.

After having them straightened manually, the operation had released the tendons and huge metal braces were put on which were near enough impossible to get on and off.

It seemed that my body didn't like the potions very much. Maybe the amount of ingredients in that last potion, the one that had made me sick, was just too much for my body to handle? One thing was for sure, I was damned if I would ever go through the withdrawal symptoms again because that had been the hardest part to handle.

CHAPTER SIXTEEN

The Central Line

The stabbing for blood continued on consecutive days. The few drops of blood they did manage to obtain showed that my blood was lacking phosphate.

Boss Man's sidekick had told me that phosphate levels can only be maintained through intravenous access. Our bodies need phosphate to be able to function effectively.

It is a mineral that forms one percent of the human body, and deficiencies in it our rare. In my case, the levels were due to starvation from the weeks of being sick so often.

Cue a visit from almost every doctor in the hospital, each one saying they would "have a little go," which was code for "I'm about to stab you with a needle and hope for the best!"

On one day, I counted that I was subjected to a whopping twenty attempts at getting a cannula in with very little success.

All these attempts caused my already fragile veins to completely shut down. Boss Man's sidekick informed me that the last person to try, before more drastic plans needed to be looked at, would be a paediatrician. Perhaps for the first time, I saw fear on the sidekick's face.

The ripple of nerves, so visible through her hazel eyes and in the way she held herself upon her small frame, was palpable in the atmosphere. Despite being a well-respected neurologist, she never even tried to take bloods from me for fear of failure. This was common because blood-taking was a rather egotistical affair for all the doctors—each wanting to better their colleagues but afraid of not succeeding.

However, as I watched her white doctor's jacket whisk away I hoped that whoever came next would get the cannula in because 'drastic measures' didn't sound like a good thing.

Half an hour later, I was awoken by a bubbly, slightly rotund paediatrician, with a kind face.

"Hi, are you Jess Taylor?"

I nodded profusely and predicted correctly his next words.

"Can I try and take some blood from you and try to get a cannula in? I will just have a look first."

He looked and then sighed deeply when no obvious opportunity presented itself. He felt my wrist and gave it just one last try using a cannula originally intended for babies. I have to admire him for admitting that his plan wasn't going to work.

"Okay Jess, I'm not going to try anymore. They will have to put you to sleep and insert one that way. Pleasure to have met you."

I stared into space whilst contemplating the next stage.

No point in worrying, I told myself, *what will be will be. At times like this, all one can do is to hang in there and keep fighting.*

Boss Man's sidekick came in with a form that needed to be signed. Maybe she had temporarily forgotten that I was unable to move and had been since coming into her care. Who knows?

She had to fax a form to Dad instead, but I didn't know the form's content. Always the last to find out.

Before long, an anaesthetist and a surgeon came to the bedside; they had obviously been in deep conversation. One of the women in scrubs looked at the other.

"We could try but I'm not overly happy about it."

"Hi Jess, here is an anaesthetist and a surgeon. They've come to see if they can help," Boss Man's sidekick said nervously.

"Let us look at her veins, just in case," said the surgeon distantly, not even having the common courtesy to acknowledge my presence.

All the surgeons I met seemed to lack the most basic people skills. They must be used to people just being asleep.

"Well I haven't done it on someone so young. I will try—"

Her buzzer went off. She checked it and ran out of the room.

"I want someone with her," noted the anaesthetist, before she also went running out of the room like a flash of lightning.

I had so much neurological pain to contend with that I barely had the energy to think about anything else. It was probably good that my mind was distracted from thinking about the words 'I want someone with her' as they hadn't made whatever was about to happen sound very appealing.

Why was nobody explaining and talking to me, human to human? Instead, I was brushed past as if I wasn't there. Staff spoke in hushed voices, glancing over at my bed with worried expressions.

It will be okay though, I reassured myself, *the lovely paediatrician said I would be put to sleep.*

Clive came into the bay. Before walking to my bedside, he stopped and tried to change his concerned face into one full of reassurance but, when he actually saw me, the reassurance vanished.

Where is my Jess? I could see him thinking.

My body was covered in marks, skin a greyish white, just skin and bones, with two enormous braces for arms.

'What happening?' I whispered in code urgently.

"They are going to get a central line into you—in your neck, your chest or down there," he pointed downwards towards his groin. "Someone will be with you."

Oh, my! I could hardly find the words for how I felt. Dad had joked before that they should go through my neck as it must be the only part of me with working veins but I wasn't laughing now. Instead, there was an unnerving tingle in my spine.

It will be okay, I told myself, *I will be asleep.*

I was bathed in a special lotion used for operations as an MRSA preventative and readied for theatre but it was fine because I was going to be asleep, just like the man had said.

They were short-staffed on the ward which meant a long wait so, as the day began to draw in, I got more and more agitated.

"You are on the list!" Boss Man's sidekick said, with slight relief in her voice.

On the list but all alone. Where was Mum? Dad? Somebody? Apparently, it was too much of an emergency for them to wait long enough for anyone familiar to get there and be with me.

I had two hours of waiting alone. I didn't even have my dark glasses because they had not returned them after the wash.

Then, the nightmare really began.

A porter called my name. I was about to go down. Where was the person who was meant to be with me?

The care assistant, who my fellow patients in the bay had nicknamed Grotbags, appeared from nowhere, thrusting the dark glasses onto me.

Grotbags was a character in a children's TV show from before my time. The other girls told me that she was a green witch, perfectly describing my current feelings for our own Grotbags.

She was in a foul mood, chatting away to the porter but taking not the blindest bit of notice of the girl she was supposed to be looking after. If she had, she would have been aware of how much discomfort I was in thanks to all the dazzling lights. It wasn't as if I could just pull the cover over my head with arms stuck rigidly by my side.

Fear was mounting up inside but I knew that it was essential for me to stay calm.

When we got to the pre-op unit, a nurse dressed in blue scrubs came bustling over to us and began to ask a series of questions, which Grotbags answered.

At least I have someone who will be there when I go to sleep, I thought. It was a small comfort.

However, after answering all the questions, she said, "Need anything else or can I go now?"

What? I was gobsmacked and began to panic. *No!* I thought desperately, *don't go!*

A feeble murmur was all that I could manage as, with horror,

I watched her leave me and bustle off. From that moment, I loathed her. We had named her Grotbags for good reason.

My bed was wheeled into the surgical room, which was a hellish place for somebody with M.E. They connected me up to a machine to measure my heart rate. The horrendously bright lights beat down on my eyes. It was like being in an episode of the hospital television show *Casualty*.

About six people towered over me, ready to slide me onto the operating table. Where was the general anaesthetic? I wasn't asleep; they had got this horribly wrong, surely? The panic was now affecting my breathing, making it come in short, sharp breaths.

Breathe slowly and deeply, I briefly heard what I thought my therapists would be saying. Funnily enough that wasn't the first thing occupying my mind.

The machines started beeping urgently as my heart rate rose. I could feel my heart pummelling in my chest. The anaesthetist arrived and she was angry.

"Where is the care worker from the ward? I told them that I wasn't prepared to do it on someone so young unless she has someone with her who knows her," she exclaimed.

"I didn't know. The carer left," one of the scrubbed up women said hastily.

"Jess," said the surgeon, talking to me for the first time and in an almost motherly way. "We can wait. Are you sure you want us to continue? It is okay to say no and we will wait for someone to come down from the ward."

A kind lady next to me gently said that she would hold my hand. It was her or the wrath of Grotbags, which would not be a pretty sight.

Why wasn't I going to sleep? My mind jerked and darted from one solution to the other. Neither looked good. I would be brave. I would try. I nodded my head for them to continue.

A clammy, cold sweat covered my body whilst I waited, completely terrified, for the next move. The machines were constantly beeping as my heartbeat continued to rocket up. I didn't know what was about to happen. How could I do this? I was scared stiff, literally.

"Okay Jess, we are going to move your head to the side," one of the surgeons said.

No, no, no, this wasn't part of the bargain. No, really! Stop now!

I tried to whisper but they weren't listening and they manually moved my head around to the left. My whole body began to shake violently and uncontrollably.

No! I panicked.

The first thing one would do when being attacked would be to protect your neck, surely? But my wretched arms were bound to my side in big metal braces.

"Just putting the local anaesthetic in."

"Ah, ah," I yelped in agony, but I was helpless to respond. I started to hyperventilate as the pain trapped me.

"And again." The second hit.

More screams whilst my neck became numb in the slowest possible way. Suddenly it dawned on me: *How am I going to be able to breathe when I can't feel my neck?* I tried to breathe but panic was taking over.

"Put something over her head," I heard one of them instruct another.

"Okay darling, we are going to put something over your head and put a weight over it so you don't have to hold your head at all," the woman looking after me said whilst placing an operating sheet over my head, with a blanket on top that which acted like a weight.

This temporarily helped with the brightness of the operating lights, as it covered my face too. There was enough space from the sheet to allow me to breath but I felt constricted. That, and them holding my head down, kept my head still at least. It was like a hunter capturing its prey, disabling the part of the body that was needed.

I was sobbing quietly but I couldn't stop my body from shaking with fear for I could not even see now. Normally, I would revel at the darkness but, in this terrifying situation, it was just another sense I had lost. I groaned and whimpered whilst they felt for my pulse.

"It will be okay, darling; you are doing so well," said the nice lady looking after me.

I was hyperventilating and tried to slow down my breathing.

"I can't feel her pulse! I can't feel her pulse, dammit!" a junior surgeon said.

I quivered involuntarily. When would this end?

"Look," the junior surgeon snapped. "The more you cry, the more likely we are to miss and then you will die."

"Not appropriate! Calm yourself down," the head surgeon said to the junior with irritation in her voice. "It's okay, Jess, we've got this."

Die? Oh, God Almighty. Die? Did she have any idea what she had just said? Keep still, keep still Jess, I thought in desperation. *I really don't want to die.*

I repeatedly sang each word of a nursery rhyme called Catch a Falling Star in my head, desperately trying to drown out the machines and people. Tears fell uncontrollably down my face.

I wasn't going to die.

"Shhh, it's okay, darling." I imagined Mum was in the room, even though it was the lady next to me who was comforting me.

Moments passed that felt like hours. The shaking started to decrease. I distantly heard the surgeons talking. The head surgeon was trying not to show her distaste over what had just been said to me. The junior surgeon looked for my pulse again but couldn't find it.

"Let me take over," the head surgeon said.

You don't want to die, Jess, I told myself.

The junior surgeon's word had punctured my insides with pure fear. My head was positioned tightly to my left; there were people on either side of my body, holding it down.

"Keep very still for me, Jess, we are going in," the head surgeon said firmly whilst prodding the area she was about to puncture.

Despite the local anaesthetic that was meant to fully numb the area, I could still feel their pokes and jabs as they stabbed the area in my neck. I let out a yelp like that of a wounded animal.

Something cold started trickling down to the back of my neck. It took a minute for me to realise that it was my own blood flowing out of me and gathering in a pool.

I imagined Gran alongside the rest of my family, instead of all these strange people with scrubs on and their mouths covered by masks. I had to dig deep, so very deep, to find something to hold on to in order to get me through this.

I saw Gran's smiling face. I brought myself back to a

moment we had shared as a family. It was Christmas, the fire was crackling. We were watching *The Snowman* as an old family tradition, smiling and laughing with one another.

Hold on, I told myself, *just hold on*.

They had pierced into my neck, like vampires. More screams of pain and horror filled the operating theatre as I continued to feel the unnatural snake making his way down my neck.

Just keep holding on, I thought.

I wasn't going to die.

Barely daring to breathe, I whimpered. The snake glided its way slowly down my neck, making me feel parts of my body that I hadn't felt in such a long time. Tears streamed down my face when the thick tube worked its way into me, moving deeper inside. It felt like my veins had suddenly become contortionists.

"Two staples here and we are done," the surgeon said. "Well done."

The local anaesthetic was beginning to wear off but just two staple shots into my neck and it was over at last.

Everything that I had held back for those critical moments came flooding to the fore. An exhaustion that surpassed all I had felt in a long time made me want to curl up in a ball and have Gran and Mum tell me that it was going to be alright.

Instead, I couldn't move my neck at all and was soon hit with the cackles of Grotbags being outrageously friendly to the porter whilst not even bothering to glance at her highly traumatised patient.

The head surgeon had decided that it was too traumatic for me to go into the recovery room, that I needed somewhere I knew, a place where the bright lights wouldn't scald my eyes.

The recovery room would only have added to the trauma that had rocked my being.

Exhaustion, pain, exhaustion, pain—my brain slowly switched between the two settings.

*

I arrived back in the bay and started to sob as the trauma of what had happened sunk in. Sweat poured down me; there was nobody in the world who deserved to go through that alone.

Boss Man's sidekick hurried into the room, pressing the buzzer immediately for help. My fellow patient, Holly, came to try and comfort me. It was a pitiful sight for her to see—a person reduced to nothing.

Grotbags walked in, responding to the buzzer, trying to look important.

"I want a nurse," Boss Man's sidekick said flatly. "Were you with her?"

"Oh, I took her down and then went back to collect her at the end. Can I help?"

"I asked for a nurse, a real nurse, now," Boss Man's sidekick said with cold authority for it had suddenly dawned on her why I was in such a state.

Clive arrived and gaped at the mess that was my bed. The sheet was covered in blood and I was shaking violently.

"Why the hell did no one stay down with her? Will you just look at her?"

His head dropped as he shook it. He explained that he hadn't even realised nobody had stayed.

How could you not? I desperately thought. *You let this happen, Clive, because you should have been the one coming down there with me. Why weren't you there?*

I was so very tired but needed to be moved to have an X-ray done, to check the new line was in the correct position.

Just give me a few seconds to close my pounding eyes, I thought and then fell into an inviting sleep, dreaming of those strange people with operating masks and hats.

When I woke up, it was late in the evening and a male doctor accompanied by a female nurse came to check my blood and start this all-important drip to hydrate me and give me that vital phosphate. He first checked the line, bringing a big 50ml syringe.

What on earth does he need that for? I thought wildly. He connected the syringe to my central line and withdrew 20ml of blood without me really noticing at all. When he flushed it, the cold could be felt all the way down my neck to my chest.

When morning came, I realised to my displeasure that it was Judgement Day and Boss Man would be making an appearance. *Gracious no*, I thought as I tried to move my head and then winced when the throbbing pain in my neck started up again.

To my utter surprise it was the other physiotherapist, Tiny, who I saw first. Exercises were on the list for today's agenda.

As much as you would assume it should be like this every day, it wasn't at all. She got started without any enquiry into how I was or discussion of what new exercises could be done now that I had a great big tube attached to the side of my neck. She just pretended it wasn't there.

In a way, I hoped that Boss Man would take a similar approach. I could just imagine the furore to come.

After Tiny left, Boss Man with his sidekick next to him, came marching into the bay, skipping all the other patients' beds to find mine on the end. My heart skipped a beat as I hated the staring crowd that always accompanied him. Once everyone was still, he cleared his throat so everyone would be paying attention to his every word.

"I say you must get off these bloody tubes! An NG tube AND a central line; I don't like this. You can remove those bloody glasses too!" He raised his voice with typical drama.

Did he not realise what had happened to me yesterday? Had I asked for a tube to be inserted in such an inhumane way?

Yet still, I found myself slightly nodding my head in unison with the murmured agreement from the crowd.

"We won't be able to keep you here like this, do you understand?" he continued in a loud and highly pronounced voice.

I will make sure I wave the magic wand too, I thought quietly,

Grotbags was revelling in every word Boss Man said and tried to continue the theme.

"Are you going to keep those glasses off?"

And without waiting for an answer, she pulled them off. It was a bright, sunny, winter's morning and I could barely open one eye.

Boss Man and his crowd moved on, and it was time for my wash. Grotbags and the other girl ignored me and spoke excitedly to one another whilst they worked. When they went to leave they did so without replacing my glasses.

Oh, come on, I thought in despair, *how much more can you put me through?* Thankfully, Clive came in.

"Give her back the glasses," he said with a sigh.

"But he said and she agreed!" Grotbags insisted.

"Ladies, ladies. slowly, yeah? Slowly," and he replaced the glasses.

I couldn't thank him enough; he had nearly made up for yesterday.

Mum and Gran came to see me soon after the central line procedure but I was so tired and unwell that it didn't feel like a visit at all. Gran held my hand.

"It's all going to get better sweetheart, I'm almost sure of it. Remember our book, Jess? What do you think? Should we go with our real names or a pen name?"

She tried desperately to distract me before she whispered in my ear, "I think of you all the time and I'm praying for you, just like the hundreds of people I've told about you, all across the world, are doing."

In that moment, it felt like God wasn't listening to anyone though. Or maybe He was on holiday that week.

I couldn't see many of my friends, just Nick, who was so incredibly loyal. He had been to see me nearly every other week, since I had come to The Promised Land, even for a short couple of minutes. He bought me a present to open.

Nick sat by my bed, and sighed. "I've got to get my act together, this present doesn't make it near to the glasses, which may I say, transformed your life. But this year was harder. How do I top last year?"

I looked at him and although he made me smile, I was really suffering. It all felt too much. I wanted to be out there choosing his present, living outside in the real world.

"I'm not sure what fragrance you like so I bought you something that you can make up your own perfume."

He wasn't aware that I had become sensitive to smell but still it meant a lot that he was doing this for me.

"Then you won't get the dreadful hospital smell!" He lowered his voice. "Babes, you've got to get out of this place. We have so much to do!"

I know Nick. I know.

I soon began to know the ins and outs of the tube stuck inside my neck. The first 20ml of blood is waste blood and you should take 50ml all together. It should be flushed with saline afterwards and then cleaned with an alcohol wipe.

Half of the doctors had no idea what they were doing. No wonder there were so many infections when the professionals didn't even know the correct routine!

I often ended up translating to my parents when something had been done wrong so they could go and find the doctor to flush it or put the lid back on! I'd be damned if I was going to get an infection due to others' stupidity.

After many days, I had reached the time to say goodbye to the central line. There was too much of a risk of infection and apparently they were not insured to keep me in this bed with one of them.

The Sister on the ward came to do the removal. She brought Clive with her so he could watch her remove it. Again, I felt like the exhibit in the museum but I didn't care if it meant getting rid of this wretched central line. She pulled the stapled stitches off my neck.

"Okay, hold your breath and don't move. One—two—three!"

On three she pulled and I felt a sudden lurch as the line, which went in as far as the beginning of my aorta, came slithering like a snake out of my vein. And it was out. I was still holding my breath, waiting for the signal from the nurse to breathe again. She pushed down hard on my neck to stop the bleeding.

"You can breathe now," she said.

Then it was over.

CHAPTER SEVENTEEN

Heartbroken

"I'm so sorry to tell you this, darling, but Gran is very, very poorly. She is on machines that are breathing for her. It happened last night."

I had been so jovial that my lovely dad had been allowed to see me during the week. Partly due to being sleepy, it hasn't occurred to me to wonder why it had been allowed, nor why he had come so late. The words froze me to the core. Not Gran, surely not?

My gran was full of life, incredibly youthful, my best friend and my second mum. She meant everything to me and more. She was such a merry spirit. A spirit like that couldn't just go. I couldn't possibly continue on through every day without her.

The news isn't good but she is still alive, I thought desperately. *Gran can pull through anything and she's always saying she hasn't got time to be ill.*

"She has had a massive heart attack, Jess. I'm so sorry to have to tell you like this," Dad continued.

No, no, no, my insides screamed, yet all I could manage was one thick teardrop that rolled down my cheek.

Dad hugged me but I felt cold; he gave me a peck on the

cheek but my cheek was numb. I was numb. Maybe it had just been a nightmare and this tragedy would be gone in the morning. Just one great big horror story. I was being irrational but I didn't care. This bed in this hospital was the last place I wanted to be.

"They are going to be finding out the—"

The machine feeding me started to beep. The enforced pause allowed me a moment to exhale and shakily inhale another breath. It was a typical hospital interruption, exactly the reason why, at that moment, I hated everything about being there, every last bit of it.

Dad continued, "We are going to find out the test results tomorrow."

I wanted to be there, back in Canterbury, with her. I wanted to hold her hand and comfort her, as she had done for me throughout my whole illness.

"'You'll let me know?" I whispered slowly and softly.

Dad would wait patiently and interpret, as I struggled to form each word. My family were able to translate all my code, whereas the hospital staff didn't have the time or patience to even try to decode.

"Yes, I will let you know, honey. I will," he assured me.

He looked at me with his big, dark eyes and a tear ran down his cheek. I saw it as an acknowledgement that I wasn't overreacting. His voice started to crackle.

"Cuppa tea, love? Hot chocolate?" the booming voice of the tea lady, Rihanna, came into the open bay.

The moment passed as quickly as it had begun. Dad looked away, wiping his face on the sleeve of his bottle-green paramedic uniform. I tried to squeeze his finger with my limp hand. I wanted that moment back but instead I got a nurse coming in to give me my night medication.

Dad looked longingly into the dark glasses, searching for my eyes, before he voiced the dreaded conclusion that accompanied the bustling nurse.

"'I think I am going to be kicked out, Jess. I will ring the ward tomorrow. I've made sure everyone is aware of what's happening."

He kissed my forehead and, as he turned to go, fresh tears ran freely down my face. I looked up at him to see his big watery eyes. One last look.

"I love you, Jess."

Even though I was surrounded by the hustle and bustle of a busy hospital, I felt as though I was the only one there. Just one person who spent that entire night praying so hard for one very special lady. Nobody could see the empty hole that I felt inside my heart. It was like an earthquake had shaken my world. The tears fell silently down my face as I relived the moment I had been told the devastating news.

*

He didn't ring. I spent all of the next day waiting for the call. Boss Man came though. He had been informed of my gran's deterioration in health, yet still he brought his booming, authoritative voice. He stood at the bottom of my bed, as if he was inspecting some unknown specimen. Short and rotund, yet immaculately dressed, he barked his latest orders and enquiries.

"I want to see a big improvement in you, otherwise I will

be sending you back to where you came from and you will never get better. You wouldn't want that, would you?" he said in a harsh tone.

I shook my head abruptly, whilst saying in my head.

Saturday came and I waited patiently for someone to come around the corner. Gran's condition lay quietly in the back of my mind. At night, I had revisited the scene of my father telling me the news.

A weary man stumbled into my room. *Dad!* My heart skipped a beat. His eyes looked exhausted and his hair was dishevelled.

"Hello darling," he started but I couldn't wait any longer.

"Gr-an?" I whispered expectantly.

His face sunk as he leant over the bed. It looked as if it took every single bit of willpower to form the next sentence.

"Oh darling, I don't know how to say. . ."

His words had told me nothing so far but I could put two and two together to realise it was not good news. It was like the whole world had stopped, waiting for the news.

"She's not going to wake up, sweetheart. I'm so sorry. The damage to her brain is so severe that she is brain dead."

I was stunned. The words had slapped me around the face. *No!* I gave a cry of anguish but no words would formulate. My whole world was smashing into pieces.

Dad gathered me up in a warm embrace and I sobbed.

"You never rang."

"How could I, Jess? How could I begin to say the news and have some random stranger tell you without being there myself?"

"I. . . want. . . to see. . . her," I whispered slowly.

"No, you don't. You wouldn't want this to be your last memory of her. She wouldn't want that, would she?"

Days upon days passed and my beautiful gran remained in a coma in a broken body.

The first time I saw Mum was a shock. She had spent every waking moment at the hospital with her own mother. Her pale complexion looked ghostly; her eyes showed deep distress and all she could do was hug me tightly.

"You are the mirror image of each other," she whispered sadly.

It was as if we were all carrying a heavy load along darkened paths. The world was losing a light, one that was once so bright and full of life but was now faded into a lifeless form.

All of this had happened a week before Christmas 2007. I had now been in hospital for over a year. Gran had loved the sparkle of Christmas, the family all together and the giving of gifts. I couldn't imagine a Christmas without her; it made me feel hollow. I knew none of my family wanted to celebrate Christmas this year, so I had to come up with something miraculous to bring even the smallest of smiles.

The only thing I could think of to do was dress up. So, my bewildered family got some friends to help me as I set about my task. Not being able to talk properly or move were big disadvantages. Needless to say, it was a struggle but it was do-able.

I was going to be the Christmas Fairy, adorned with sparkles and glitter. Gran would like that. Or rather, Gran would have liked that. Gran would not be there; she was still in a coma that she wouldn't wake from, but she was not dead.

In some ways, it made the days longer, the pain more

apparent, as we carried her alongside us. Christmas came and went. It had been anything but special. My fairy outfit was the only thing that brought a smile to Mum's face.

I wished that my magic wand, which lay across my broken body, could magic this nightmare away from us.

No such luck, I realised, whilst I was spoon-fed grotesque, puréed Brussels sprouts. *Tasty! Not.*

It was the start of trying to ween me off the NG tube. I was still being fed through that tube but the plan was to introduce new flavours to improve my swallow.

With a heavy heart, I knew the inevitable was going to happen and Gran would pass away. Although this tore my heart apart, the waiting game was even more torturous.

Two weeks had passed but it had felt like two years. Part of me wanted her to pass away before New Year. I was too exhausted to speculate whether this was selfish thinking or not. I knew she was no longer the empowering lady she once was and that she never would be again.

Even as I write this, tears break through like lava breaking out of an erupting volcano.

On New Year's Day 2008, just as Tom walked onto the bay to see me at The Promised Land to hold my hand, Mum was sat in Gran's hospital room in Canterbury, holding hands with her own father and brother, having dropped my sister in the chapel of the Canterbury Hospital. Gran took her last breath. Mum's uncontrollable, hysterical sobs filled the rest of the night.

CHAPTER EIGHTEEN

A Girl Behind Dark Glasses

Progress was a constant battle that I entered into every single day. If I didn't show some sign of progress every week then my funding would not be renewed. The greater problem was my Primary Care Trust (the people with the money) did not know what else to do with me.

At first, I was simply too ill for them to figure out what their definition of progress was. It was certainly different to what I considered it to be. I had to show I was worth the money they were paying. It was like being in a circus performing to these people with the money bags.

I had become a puppet the moment the M.E. Monster had entered my life. Not through want, quite the opposite, the M.E. Monster was the mysterious puppeteer who controlled my jerking body. Money—that thing the world revolved around—was my other puppeteer.

I was often threatened with being shoved back to where I came from unless there was progress. If only it was that easy. Scarecrow did not seem to understand the sheer torture my body was going through every moment of every day, even though she was supposed to be a specialist.

Light sensitivity was the first thing they wanted to overcome. Boss Man had made this as clear as rain. I did whatever I could to please him, otherwise Judgement Day would be even more horrendous and scary.

I had to show them that I was putting up a good fight. Personally, I felt that having some food go down me orally was more important but the doctors had their own ideas. I followed the doctors' orders because I still believed that the doctors would make me better and, despite being scary in his persona, Boss Man was the doctor of all doctors.

Boss Man walked in to the beat of my hammering heart. I could hear the leather soles click-clack, click-clack on the hard floor. Whilst another patient got examined, I tried to think of some positive changes that I could achieve, something that would please him, but I had just had a central line removed and was not in a position to make any other immediate changes.

I hated to think it, let alone say it, but I had nearly not made it on several occasions, thanks to the M.E. Monster, and my only way to get through the situation was to think for the moment and no further ahead.

A day at a time, I thought, *that's my only option*.

Boss Man arrived and his words were plain and simple. 'A great improvement' was something that I would have liked too, but whilst real life continued on around me, I didn't know how that was going to be possible.

The fact that my beloved gran had just died meant nothing to him. He wanted progress and that was all that he cared about. Did he not realise the reality of my condition? Apparently, because I was younger, he got more upset about what was happening to me and would express his passion and helplessness as anger.

Yes, we should all be angry at the situation, angry at the complete injustice, angry at how ill this disease can make someone whilst no research is being done into M.E. and its different severities. I get that. I really do, because I feel angry on occasions too. But angry at me? Isn't that completely counter-productive? I thought in exhaustion.

Scarecrow came up with a plan to get rid of the dark glasses. It didn't matter if I felt able to do it or not, I had to try—for my darling gran and for myself.

I shuddered at the idea of me being a sixteen-year-old, slumped over a walking aid like some old biddy. I was here to get better! I was missing out on home life and being with Becky. I was on a mission to get better.

If only it were that simple. I had come to learn that life was never that simple for anybody, let alone me.

By this point, I had been moved to a different bay, right by the small window. Access to the night sky allowed my imagination to run wild and I started to think up fairy tales in which the stars outside would take me home. . .

The next day was the start of 'Operation Remove the Glasses,' as they were peeled off me by Scarecrow.

"Look at me," she demanded, as I screwed my eyes up tightly to block out the shock from the rush of light. The sudden stimuli had really rocked me. "Open your eyes, Jess."

I heard her voice but felt blinded by the light that infiltrated the backs of my eyes, even though they were closed tightly.

"Jess, look at me!" she said in an exasperated tone.

I took a few moments to compose myself. I peeled back a scrunched-up eyelid and couldn't help but yelp.

"Ah! Ah! Ah!" I yelped. Shock. Searing agony. Bright light flooding in.

Help. In a split second I was gone. My eyes were closed again.

What the hell was that? Was that how I was going to see from now on? Comprehension fast eluded me, utter agony filled me. My insides squirmed and screamed in pain as my M.E. Monster cackled at me.

Scarecrow seemed to have completely missed my response, somehow she had missed the anguish on my face as it screwed up like a contortionist, for she ordered that the glasses be removed for two hours.

"You will be fine. You should be doing this," she said coolly.

I should be doing this, I thought, exhausted from my efforts and with an insistent headache throbbing in the background.

I can remember her showing me a mirror one time. She wouldn't allow me to look into it unless the dark glasses were removed.

"Ah! Ah! Ah!" I yelped.

I hadn't seen a mirror in over a year; I had no idea what I looked like. For the first time, as I squinted, I saw a sickly, pale girl with dark hair. She had a tube stuck to the side of her face. I didn't recognise myself. I had forgotten what I looked like. I was too ill to take any notice or any interest.

It was just a split second and my eyes felt like sharp nails were scratching down them but I had seen my face for the first time—that was my sort of progress. But it wasn't good enough or quick enough for Boss Man.

Two hours felt like a lifetime to keep my eyes open but I had no choice—I had to get better.

Holly came over to me on her way to the bathroom. I could

sense someone was there. I screwed up my eyes and pushed to open them and I screamed.

"You are doing so well, Jess." I could hear Holly's soft voice but I couldn't concentrate on the words as, internally, I squirmed in sheer agony.

Tears reached my eyes but did not fall. They stayed in place, trying to soothe my stinging eyes.

I needed to press my buzzer to get some help so I moved my head to click the buzzer. Someone came but I had no idea who it was. I flashed open my eyes. Once again, I felt the soaring pain.

I had been able to make out the figure of a short person running along. I opened my eyes again. The carer tried to help but couldn't comprehend my disorientation.

It was not long before the hallucinations had started. Numbers would fall down my field of vision like numbers in *The Matrix*. I tried getting rid of them by moving my head but every time I opened my eyes, they would continue to fall—in the colours you get when you've just looked at something bright and then close your eyes.

Then, to my horror, other things started to join these strange numbers—people, objects flashing in and out of my vision. It was distressing because there was no way out, and no time out either.

I tried to code to Scarecrow; she was anything but sympathetic. She tried to tell me that it might be because I was lonely.

What? Lonely? Come on, I can't be seeing numbers just because I am lonely.

On this occasion, Boss Man corrected her. "Of course, you

are seeing things," he said in a matter-of-fact voice. "Your eyes *need* light to function and, because you are stopping light getting to them via these bloody glasses and this darkened room, of course you will have your eyes tricking you!"

Well that was that, I sighed.

Over time, my eyes slowly adjusted but never fully got used to the sharp, piercing brightness of daylight or the bright lights that glared at me from the ceiling. The irony was people thought this was a darkened room!

It took many months and my dark glasses became my reward for doing well and managing to go without them for two hours.

I remember using my muffled sounds to tell Scarecrow of my plans to write a book. I told her the title.

"What was that? Couldn't you come up with something more positive?" she said in a moaning voice.

A Girl Behind Dark Glasses is who I am. I cannot lie to people and pretend I am something that I am not. This is my life and people need to know about it. One day, my story could be the basis for change so no other person has to go through this hell. That's something extremely positive, isn't it?

Our differences in opinion couldn't have been more obvious but one day I would be flying free from this. On that day, I would have a book in shops, my name on its cover, and I would have done my bit to help make a difference. That is what fuelled me every day that I battled against the M.E. Monster.

It was the hope that filled me every time I tried to write my name and succeeded. Okay, it looked a little better than a toddler's attempt but even holding a pen was progress for me.

In my head, I listened to the music from *The Lord of the Rings*. The music that plays when Frodo gets to the end of his battle with the One Ring and Aragorn takes his army on one last charge to victory. I imagined my own body, my own willpower, were battling the dreaded M.E. Monster.

Instead of crying, "For Frodo!" We shouted, "For Jess! We shall fight this day for Jess; I fight with you and we shall not wait for a tomorrow to fight this beast! We may be outnumbered but we are not outnumbered in our own minds. Together we fight!"

With that, all the antibodies inside my body went to war alongside me and, in my reverie, we won.

CHAPTER NINETEEN

The Five Stages of Grief

In my quiet dream state, I visited Bluebell Hill with Gran. We walked along the cliff, picking wild roses and laughing with one another. We travelled along the White Cliffs of Dover too, the wind playing with my hair, as we watched the ferries coming and going from the port. Together again, at peace.

Various chaplains and other people had tried to explain death to me but they all got stuck on why it had to happen in the first place.

"God needed an angel," was the only response from many of them.

He has got Himself one beautiful angel then, I thought.

The conciliatory words were just muffled by my pain-ridden body anyway. My light sensitivity had increased but I had stayed true to my resolve since Boss Man had visited with his fear-inducing, "I want to see a big improvement in you, otherwise I will be sending you back to Sunshine Ward. You wouldn't want that, would you?"

To stay true to my word, I had to pull something out of the bag. I needed to do something miraculous because I had heard him shout on many occasions and it was not a fun experience.

Even though my body felt ever more drained, slowly strangled by a soft blanket of exhaustion, and the nerve pain pushed my tolerance to the limits, I still fought on.

"The sunglasses have to go for good," Scarecrow said so I relinquished the sunglasses.

The first time was hellish to say the least! My eyes were screwed up tightly. The flashes of light viciously scalding my eyeballs.

Holly would come over to visit me from her cubicle and I could barely see her shape. She treated me with kindness and poured encouragement on the monumental effort I was making, telling me how well I was doing.

Although it came at a cost, it was still incredible to see actual solid improvement. I had to teach my body how to see again but the light didn't agree with my eyes. The headache that came with it was something chronic.

The final goodbye to Gran at her funeral was nearing. I dreaded it. I didn't want to let go; I wasn't ready for that. Maybe it was the fact that I would have to imagine the funeral, as I wasn't even able to get out of the hospital.

Becky was withdrawn, she sat by my side, gazing around. A tear falling every so often. Tom put on a brave face and held onto Mum. The real shock came when I first saw Grandad after it had happened.

I let out a sob, as he walked into the cubicle, and Gran did not follow. He was a shadow of himself. His whole world had shattered into pieces but there was no fixing it now. He tried to comfort me, but there were no words that could ease my heartache.

On the day, I wore something sparkly and I had a card to

open from Mum because she knew I would be alone, as it was a week day.

Dearest Jess,

The pain of losing my beloved Mummy and your amazing Gran is immeasurable. For all the things that describe Gran, I think the one word that sums it up is selfless. If only God could tell me why it had to happen like that but then we wouldn't want her to suffer anymore, would we? Gran has done so many wonderful things for us all that it is time for her to be treated now. Feel this hug coming through this card to you, my baby. Stay strong today. I love you to the stars and beyond,

Mummy x

Even though I couldn't attend in person, I still felt like I had been there, as I had written a poem to be read at the service. Becky had listened whilst I whispered it to her, noting it down word for word.

My thoughts returned to the White Cliffs of Dover and how the ferries slowly moved towards the horizon, getting smaller and smaller, until they disappeared. Those ships didn't actually disappear though. They just moved over my horizon and onto a new one.

Maybe this was the best way to understand death: she had not gone but had entered a new horizon. It seemed a logical explanation to me.

When Boss Man visited just a day and a half later, he was not satisfied. Not satisfied that despite my grief I had pushed hard to be free of the dark glasses for a few hours, which, as Holly had said, was a huge deal.

He visited the other patients first. I always felt anxious when he came; I was not a fan of his booming voice and it did nothing for my ME.

Having the fear of God put into me was exhausting. His leather clip-clop shoes made their way over to my bed. With him was the physiotherapist, Tiny. There was also Boss Man's sidekick plus various others, probably including occupational health professionals and student doctors.

I was too ill to take in those kind of details. His thundering tones arrived on cue. I was expecting some form of congratulations for my efforts and empathy towards my situation. Who was I kidding?

"You may have been going through some difficult times, but here it is different. We don't have the luxury of taking time to grieve. Move on—you must improve," he bellowed.

I was stunned. He didn't even say what benchmark he wanted. He just expected more and more improvements. Anger bubbled inside of me. *How dare he? How could he?*

He moved away from my bed to carry on a conversation with one of the doctors and then just left. That's right, he just left, with no thought for the consequences of his actions or for the girl he had just immensely put down.

Fury boiled up inside me; I waited for him to walk out of the bay and then released an uncontrollable sound. Grief-stricken sobs reverberated around the bay, they were the loudest sound to come out of me since I had been hospitalised.

I was angry with him in a way that I had never been with any other person. I felt so humiliated that Boss Man had said such cruel things in front of a room full of people with no care for the effect his words would have on another human being.

My gran hadn't deserved to be dismissed like this! She was dead with no voice of her own for Christ's sake.

Soon, two carers came to my rescue, one of them was a man called Jackson. The lady hugged and comforted me but Jackson just stood there. I didn't really take much notice of him to begin with.

"Ignore that doctor, babe," the lady said with her East London accent. "Keep your head held high. He ain't got nothing on you."

The counsellor came to see me as soon as she got back from her holiday to find that my gran was no longer with us. She came with a chart held closely to her, it was titled 'The Five Stages of Grief.'

I was already familiar with the stages of grief. All I really wanted to tell her was that I was just heartbroken, nothing more and nothing less.

"The first stage is disbelief, where you question or choose to believe that it didn't happen. The second stage is blaming: sometimes yourself or even the person who has died," she said enthusiastically. "You know the 'Why did you have to leave me? How could you leave me?' The third is depression: just feeling sad, you know, and really low. The fourth is anger, being angry at the person who has left you. The last one is acceptance that the person in question is no longer with us. You can switch between them and there is no right or wrong way to go through the stages. It should take a year to eighteen months."

Acceptance was a far, distant place that I couldn't even see, let alone reach.

CHAPTER TWENTY

The Secret Truth

My body ached and hurt right down to every fibre of my being. This was my everyday state but sometimes it became too much to handle. I would watch the ticking clock and look at the small picture of Gran. She was by my side, I was sure of it, and it made the pain slightly easier to handle.

Jackson started to visit my bay more often. He was a strange man and looked as if he was a gangster of some type with his greasy hair slicked back into a ponytail, his scarred oily face and the stench of cigarette smoke that hung about him. He was a small Asian guy—one who you would pick out quite easily in a crowd.

When the nurses were doing my medication, putting it down the NG tube, Jackson would be there even though this was not his job.

When I needed the toilet, it was a massive rigmarole. Firstly, it required two carers to be free; then my dead weight had to be rolled over so I could be put onto a bedpan. There would be a wait for me to finish, before rolling me back over, so I could be cleaned up. More often than not, Jackson would be there, just watching not helping.

At first I didn't really notice. I may have been sixteen but I was a naïve little girl really; socially I was child-like. An air of innocence surrounded me. I had yet to do the normal things someone else my own age would be doing: discovering boyfriends, going on dates, having crushes. These things didn't exist in my world.

I was an exhibit that people came to see, rather than someone growing into a young woman. Jackson knew this and it made it better for him.

I tried not to let it happen—I promise I did, I really did, but my efforts were in vain. I wasn't just some pretty airhead who knew what to expect. I wasn't ready to deal with something like this. Jackson knew though; he was no airhead either.

Get to her whilst she is struggling. It's the perfect time to pounce, he must have thought.

I need you to know the effort it takes for me to write this— the tears and pain that go with it, the embarrassment that creeps over my body. The shame is suffocating but I have to tell you. I have to write it. You've journeyed with me for so long. You deserve to know the full story. I keep telling myself this.

After Gran had passed away, I was even more vulnerable than before. Not only was I mute and unable to move, but I was emotionally fragile. Jackson knew this; it must have been part of his plan.

It started one evening. I was trying to get my teeth brushed. That's all. The male carers and nurses were lazy on this ward, apart from Clive, but all the women were busy. It was late and not long before the day staff would be going home. There was no chance that the night staff would do my teeth for me. Finally, I got Jackson to help me. My biggest mistake.

Naturally, it was dark and my curtain was pulled around my little room. The other patients were resting behind their closed curtains. The only way I had of signalling when I wanted something was through moving my mouth and making different noises. A click was for a drink, my teeth chomping together was for my teeth to be brushed.

I could whisper words slightly but my voice wasn't strong enough to be heard across the room. Having your teeth brushed by somebody else is always a difficult job so I would use my tongue to point where to go. That is where it began.

"Did your boyfriend teach you that?" he asked laughing.

I didn't answer. I was confused and didn't know what he meant.

He squeezed my hand and repeated himself.

"Did your boyfriend teach you that?"

Not knowing what to do, I lay there, motionless, thinking of what on earth he could mean, but realising I had little time to answer him.

"You know, Jess, we are friends, aren't we?"

When I didn't answer him again, he tugged harder on my hand. "Aren't we?" This time his voice was harsh.

I nodded.

"So, did your boyfriend teach you that?" His eyes came alive when he repeated the same motion with his tongue that I had done but his was more pronounced.

I was confused; maybe he was talking about kissing? So I nodded.

He laughed. "Your boyfriend would ask for that? You had sex?"

I shook my head vigorously. I was sixteen for Christ's sake and had been ill since fourteen. Who the hell did he think I was?

"You've had boyfriends though? Come on, Jess, you tell your friends the truth, don't you?"

His thick accent made him sound like a gangster as well as looking like one. He brought his face right up to mine with one hand placed near my chest and he moved his tongue up and down quickly like a snake, close enough to feel his breath but without actually touching me. The stench of cigarette smoke filled my nostrils and I shook my head whilst yelping and he pulled away quickly, laughing, mocking me.

"You good at sucking?" He laughed again. What was this foreign language? What the hell did he mean?

"But you were the one that taught me that, Jess. You know." He repeated the tongue motion in a sexual way. "You were the one who taught me."

After he left, I started to question myself. My cheeks must have been scarlet red for I could feel them burning as it dawned on me what he had meant. *Oh God, no.*

A good few days passed by but I could still replay the event in my mind. Each time I thought of it, I would seize up. Being a young girl, I thought everything was my fault; how did I let this happen? Should I not have mentioned the kissing?

It didn't stop there though; now Jackson was everywhere. When I had bedpans, he was there. When I needed feeding, he was there. When I was resting, he was there.

Anytime he could, he would make the tongue motion then point for me to do it back to him. I tried not to do it but his grip around my hand would get tighter and I was scared, so I would end up doing it back. Then I would feel disgusted with myself and the whole vicious circle would repeat.

He put the fear of God into me. His mood would change

with every moment of the day. I didn't want to do it anymore. I knew that when I was being washed, he had been there and there was no way he hadn't looked at that in a sexual way.

"But you were the one who taught me that, Jess."

The mind games had already started. Who could I speak to when all I had was the Scarecrow and Boss Man? I also had the disadvantage of not being able to speak more than a few words. This also prevented me from telling my family; I couldn't explain it in few enough words and already felt a guilt that made me go clammy.

On one occasion, I lay there feeling disgusting as Jackson started stroking my hair and rubbing my shoulder getting closer and closer to my breast. Then his mood turned like a flick of a switch and he picked up a perfume bottle. He took the lid off and horror filled me when I saw him bring it closer and closer to my mouth.

"Drink it."

I moved my head from side to side. Seeing me struggle seemed to give him a bizarre thrill. I could see it in his eyes.

Please no, please, I frantically thought, as the perfume scent became unbearably strong. I looked around but there was nowhere to go, no one to see.

Help me! I cried out in my mind. I couldn't speak out loud for fear of the perfume ending up in my mouth. There was nowhere to turn; I would have to succumb to this hell.

Then, Holly came around the corner, on her way to the bathroom which was opposite my bed. As quick as a flash, the bottle was moved out of sight. She was my saving grace.

"But you were the one who taught me that, Jess."

I saw less and less of Tiny and Tall, my physiotherapists.

It had been like that for a while but the less I saw of them the more windows of opportunity it gave to Jackson.

Tall was actually the head of the physiotherapy team looking after me but I didn't feel able to tell him what Jackson was doing either. It was something I had to bottle up and just carry on with. It was, after all, my fault and there seemed to be no end to it, no way out.

Next, it was the mouthwash. He picked it up and took the lid off. I guessed what was about to happen and I was right. He brought the mouthwash over and tried to force me to drink it. It never got easier; the fear never went away but I was formulating a plan to get me out of this hell. I just had to keep thinking of the plan.

"Drink it, Jess."

This time the curtains were open. He was becoming more confident about what he dared do and when, pouncing on every moment like an animal on its prey. I moved my head from side to side. My body was shaking with fear and anticipation. I let out a groan. He squeezed my hand.

At that moment, the drugs trolley came into the bay and he loosened his grip, letting out a hearty laugh, but Holly had seen. Now Holly knew something wasn't right. But it was not as easy as just getting Holly to speak to someone. She didn't know the full facts and I couldn't tell her them either.

When dinner came that day, he threw the tray onto my table before storming out angrily. I was getting better at swallowing but the NG tube was still my main calorific intake. It scared me because his moods were changing by the hour. *What would he do next?*

He came back to feed me. Why no other carer would take

up this job was beyond me. He did the tongue action, which made me go cold inside.

"But you were the one who taught me how to do that, Jess," were the only words I could hear.

Clive came over to do my medication. He started talking to Jackson over the top of me in a different language. Only God knew what they were saying.

I began to think that maybe God was trying to help me. I had been feeling that He must be against me, or that I had done something wrong to deserve what was happening, but, every time I had come close to full-blown disaster, something had happened to prevent the inevitable. Just a little something, but maybe I should be grateful for small mercies.

Then Clive left and it was back to Jackson, as he whispered into my ear, touching me again.

"You know that is what friends do. They love each other like I love you," he said.

You bastard. You complete bastard. Only people who really love someone use those words. How can you begin to say such a thing, when I'm just your prey? This is not love.

Now, whenever anybody says, "I love you," I can hear his voice, feel the emptiness in the words that were once so precious.

CHAPTER TWENTY-ONE

The Power of Speech

Re-educating my body was a tough ask but the only way that I would be able to get out of Jackson's reach was to learn how to talk again. It was imperative. It wasn't just that I didn't have the energy to speak. It had been so long now that I had lost the ability to as well. I practised my words every night. I needed out so badly.

"But I love you, Jess."

I was doing something about the terrible situation with Jackson but I still felt a tremendous sense of guilt thanks to the sick and twisted mind games he played.

It was almost as if he sensed my new resolve to put an end to his abuse because, whilst he groomed my hair and touched my arm, he began whispering, "No one would believe you, Jess. I mean why would they believe you?"

Don't listen, I thought, as my insides squirmed at his touch. *Just get through it.*

"But I love you, Jess."

To him, I was a puppet, and he pulled the strings. People were noticing now, because he couldn't restrain himself. There was talk and questions within the bay. They could sense that something was wrong but they didn't know enough to say something other than Jackson was spending an awful lot of time with me.

I practised whispering a sentence until it was no longer too exhausting and then I would add to it. I was determined to be talking freely as soon as possible; I had to talk because I was beginning to fear Jackson's next move.

There was another obstacle looming ahead of me that needed to be overcome first: I needed to somehow get rid of Scarecrow. The shame was such that I just wouldn't be able to tell her what was happening.

She was not the type you opened up to easily. In my eyes, she was cold-hearted—the kind of woman who gloated about all that she had to a girl who had so little in comparison and no means of escape.

"No one will believe you, Jess. Why would they believe you?" Jackson's voice loomed into my mind, as I relived his words.

We are brought up in a society that believes we should speak up when wrong things are done. There are adverts on the television, various helplines that we can call for guidance. The reality is not so simple. Maybe I expected too much in my perfect little life before M.E. and trusted too much in the system to protect me in the way it promised.

It was going to be a huge gamble to expose myself in such a way and let somebody else into my private, closed-off world. It could go one of two ways.

"My. . . name. . . is. . . Jess," I started to bring the words together.

A mixture of grief and desperation accelerated my learning to talk process. I put all my energy into it.

Months passed by, months of constant abuse that was starting to escalate, as I had imagined it would.

"My name. . . is Jess."

It still sounded like a fractured whisper but was getting better.

I tried to change it around without thinking too much.

"Jessica is. . . my name."

It was fatiguing me into not being able to cope with much of the passive movement but I decided it was my only way out.

"How are you?" I said, it was in one breath and much louder than my weak whispers. How exciting!

Finally, in April I could piece together more than just one sentence. The first time I spoke to someone else, the words came out in a babble, as I desperately tried to get some of the many truths out of my overloaded brain. I wanted to correct all the things they had said that were wrong.

It may have seemed like a miraculous moment, and very uncharacteristic of a severe M.E. sufferer, but no one could have understood how long it had taken to build up to this moment.

I savoured each moment of finally being able to tell my version of events, of being able to explain M.E. from my perspective. I delighted in every word and a deep sense of pride came from my achievement. It would take a while to be able to tell someone about Jackson though, whoever that someone would be.

I pleaded. I shouted. I cried. I wanted to get rid of Scarecrow that much. I needed someone who I trusted to stop this abuse from happening. I needed help to get better.

In fact, there were so many things I needed that fuelled my desire to get away from her. They kept telling me that it was part of life to not always get who you wanted and I had to learn to live with that. But they didn't realise what was fuelling my determination for change.

Finally, I made a breakthrough and got what I needed. A replacement for Scarecrow. Hopefully, I would have someone that I could trust and speak in confidence about what was happening to me.

The new lady was a heart-warming, kind-looking woman. She liked to paint nails and do fun, girly things. She was a bit of a scatterbrain, whizzing from place to place as if she were a tornado. Her hair was short and her eyes were bold. She was pretty against her rather stocky build and wasn't one to stick to the rules. Perfect!

"Nobody would believe you, Jess. Why would they believe you?"

Jackson's words niggled inside of me. He could be right or he could be wrong. So many times, I lay there as he stroked my arms and shoulder, bringing his hand across to my chest.

He continued to force me to do things I didn't want to do. His mind games continued to silence me even though my voice was growing. I was too scared to say no to his wishes. Telling someone was a risk but it was a risk that I had to take. I knew he was going to be angry. What would happen to me? To him? In the future? Or were his words correct? Would they not believe me?

One thing was for sure, I was getting more confident now. *"But I love you, Jess."*

The four girls on the bay at that time were all pretty close with one another. Now that I could talk back, everything had changed. I was finally a fully engaged part of this family.

The NG tube was coming to the end of its usefulness. I

was making a good attempt at eating more solid meals. Finally, things were looking up for my health but I was still weighed down by Jackson. He was still growing in confidence about what he could get away with.

One day, the curtains around my bed were fully open and everybody was eating lunch. This time he chose the wrong moment to start.

"You know, Jess, sex in your country is different. You've had sex haven't you?"

"No, Jackson, of course not," I said, already embarrassed as the girl opposite started to look over curiously. It was the first time I had answered him back.

"But you've done stuff, you know." He made that same tongue action. "What age did you lose your virginity? Thirteen? Fourteen? Girls lose it young over here." A grin appeared on his evil face.

"How long have you been a carer?" I interjected, deliberately not answering his question.

"Do you think I want this for a job? Cleaning other people's arses? I was in finance in my country. I hate it over here."

"Why are you a carer then?" I was perplexed by the extreme career change.

"You have to have a certain certificate in this country. I have children to support; my little girl is three. Anyway, stop asking me questions, okay," he said flippantly.

Oh, bloody hell. The scumbag has kids. I hated to imagine what he might put that poor three-year-old through.

He left when another carer asked him to help elsewhere, thank God.

It was left for Susie, a deeply religious girl, to utter in

disbelief, "That's not right. I knew something wasn't right with him but I couldn't work out what. You need to tell someone."

I began to explain to the girls the secret truth that I hadn't been able to tell a living soul. They looked disgusted; Holly gasped and put her hand over her mouth.

"Thank you for believing me," I said relieved.

That night, Jackson and a female carer came into my room again; all the curtains were pulled. I needed a bedpan so he rolled me onto it but, when he took me off, he started to hug me against him from my hips down. Alarm bells and sirens went off inside my head.

He is about to go to the next, dreaded, hideous stage. He lay me back down as normal; the other female carer had turned the other way and completely missed what he had done.

I was breathing with short and sharp breaths. Tomorrow, I would have to tell them everything.

CHAPTER TWENTY-TWO

Justice Gone Wrong

"But who would believe you, Jess?" The malicious voice of Jackson pierced my mind.

I had told the new lady what had been happening, which had resulted in the ward manager coming hurriedly around to find out the story. Jackson had been suspended, pending further investigation.

The girls who I shared a room with had also written statements with their therapists about what they had seen. Child protection became involved for the most fleeting of moments.

I was free though. It was over; the great burden I had carried for so long now began to lift and he couldn't touch me again. I had to tell my parents, this was the part I had been dreading the most. They were asked to come and visit me. They had no idea what it was all about; nothing could have prepared them for the truth.

As they sat either side of me, my insides squirmed. Then the story came out. I said it like I was reading the words on autocue, not daring to stop for fear of the tears that were threatening to cascade down my face. Would they be angry that I hadn't told them before? Would they understand that I couldn't have told them? It would break Mum's already fragile state and I felt so guilty for that.

"Oh, my baby, my baby," Mum said, her voice coming out in a whimper. She held my body against hers. "No, no, no! Not my baby."

"What have you been going through, darling? I just. . ." Dad broke off, words failing him. But he held my hand tightly.

"I'm so sorry," I said repeatedly.

"For what, my beauty?" They both said in unison.

"For not telling you beforehand; you have to understand—I couldn't. I mean I had to keep going, because it just wasn't simple." My words were in a jumbled mess.

It is the hardest thing to tell the people who truly love you something that you know will break them into pieces. They felt that they had failed me, especially Mum. She believed she failed her daughter, failed to protect me against the evils of the world. She wrote to me, like Gran used to.

To my baby,

There are some things in life that cannot be foreseen. I promised you that I would never let you be in harm's way and I failed you. I am so sorry and can only hope that the scumbag who did this to you will rot in hell. I want to be with you right now and tell you that everything will be okay. I can only trust that Gran is protecting you until I am allowed to come and see you. It breaks me in half. I love you so much, never forget that, my darling one.

Your loving Mummy xxx

"Why would they believe you, Jess?"

There was nothing they could have done to prepare me for the events that followed. The crash, the fall that was to come. I came to dread seeing the ward manager because it was always about Jackson.

The next time he came to see me, he sat nervously by the bed with the curtains open wide.

"Well, he has been found not guilty; there just wasn't enough evidence. You know it might have been different if he had done something a bit bigger."

It would have been better if he had raped me? Is that what I am being told? He needed to have raped me before they would do anything?

It was my word against his, despite me having three witnesses. Unlike some other services, the NHS seems to go all out to protect their staff over their patients. Jackson had played the racial discrimination card too; he knew what he was doing.

The ward manager continued to speak but I only picked up occasional words for the initial shock had winded me. Jackson had got away with it. Where was the justice? He had got away with it. I tried to master myself, control the feelings of utter disgust.

"You have to understand it from his point of view. He has been cleared and needs to work so he will be working back on the ward. If we get a hint that he has done anything. . ."

This couldn't be happening. It was madness! Let the man who had been assaulting and harassing me come back onto the ward? How on earth would I ever feel safe? The overriding headache and tiredness I had been feeling before the ward manager arrived were replaced with emptiness.

"I've told all the staff so they will be looking out for any suspicious behaviour."

I fell back into his words with a bump. Now everybody knew? I hadn't wanted anybody to know about my dirty secret but now I lay there with a banner over my head saying nice and clearly, 'I've been sexually abused.' People would look at me differently, trying to suss out whether I had told the truth or was just some fibbing kid. I felt betrayed. Lost.

I can't stay here, I thought wildly.

"Who would believe you, Jess, over me?" The snarling voice of Jackson rang in my ear.

Once I told my parents, a protective blanket wrapped itself around me. Dad went absolutely mental. He wrote acid-filled letters to the head of the departments and the chief executive of the ward. It wasn't going to happen to his baby, not again. I could see the determination in his eyes.

Although Dad didn't manage to change the outcome of the disciplinary hearing, he at least managed to get Jackson off the ward. The scumbag could go and work somewhere else for as long as I was on this ward.

Time never stops, it never slows and before long I had to focus on my health again, on me, not him. The girls who had supported me wholeheartedly through the trauma had left. I felt bitterly disappointed that I was now mostly with new people who didn't understand what I had been through. It was just Holly and me for a few more months before she, too, would go.

One day, a carer came into my bay to brush my teeth and wash my face.

"You know, once, Jackson was with me and he started doing disgusting things to the door in front of a patient; I thought something funny was going on. He had even been banned from going into one lady's cubicle," she said flippantly.

"Did you ever report it?" I asked, knowing the answer already.

"Well no, not really. I just thought he was playing some sick joke," she replied feebly.

"So, he's gone and done it before but got away with it because there was no past history, when actually there was. Great." I sighed with frustration.

From the moment I spoke up, my life changed. For a brief time I thought everything was going to be alright, that I had done the correct thing. But now I was the girl who had stopped the male nurses and carers from coming into the bays.

Even Tall would keep the curtain open when he was passively moving me. In their eyes, it was my fault that they were being treated with caution. These people were not my friends; they wanted nothing to do with me anymore. I felt like an outsider.

To add insult to injury, the team looking after me wanted rid of me now too. As soon as news of the abuse had come out, they wanted me gone.

Months passed when I was oblivious to them searching for a new place for me. It can't have looked good on Boss Man's records. Not only had I not walked out of there magically cured, but I had been abused in his care, too. That must have affected his statistics somewhat. Isn't it terrible that a doctor thought like that? Boss Man only cared for his statistics, it seemed.

*

I needed a voice and I needed a friend that could be there all the time. The weeks were so long, made all the longer for knowing I was unwanted. I also needed a way to remember every detail of what was happening as my previous dealings had shown.

A phone was out of the question because I couldn't reach my face with my hand. Surely, it was not healthy to lie on my own all week, to have just one visit. I was young and I needed some form of youthful input.

Nick came every other week; I watched him grow into a young man, ready for university, but I didn't seem to grow with him.

When Nick visited me, he came in with a grin on his face.

"I got into Cambridge University, babes! Isn't that amazing? I've come with a gift for you. It will be the first and only time I get sentimental, but look."

He placed a teddy on my hospital table, with a jumper on that had an embroidered message, "Jess, you are my best friend."

A tear ran down my face, as he looked for approval in his gift.

"Even though I am going away, I will always be with you. Right there with that teddy."

He pointed at it with one hand, whilst squeezing me with his other hand. I nodded and smiled, even though my heart was breaking at the fact I wouldn't see him as often. Everyone was moving on except me.

All my old friends were busy partying and Louise was doing wild experiments with her hair. I had matured too, but in a totally different way. There had to be a way of reaching them but I had no pen and paper to write on and I could barely even write my name. I had persevered at getting better at writing though.

Dad brought in some of my old school books to show people the person I was before illness had struck—the full picture, rather than the blank canvas that M.E. had stripped me down to.

I looked at them with nostalgia, rather missing the fourteen-year-old me who hadn't realised how lucky she was just to be able to walk and move.

Amongst the books, I saw a smaller diary-sized book, the pages covered with deep purple ink—*Dear Bug*. I felt the paper that was imprinted with every thought that had ever been written there and I connected to it. I got Dad to read the beginning so I could hear the words again.

That was what was missing in my life—a diary! I didn't care that the team here had been the ones who had stopped me from writing one. I wanted to achieve something.

Speech should be an empowering tool, not one that suppresses you. I needed to find a physical Bug and then came the idea of a Dictaphone. Something that I could hold and talk to. Genius!

I got the microphone strapped onto my vest top and, whenever I wanted to or more importantly was in a state of health to be able to, I could talk to Bug.

Maybe it would become something of interest that would reach the outer world beyond this one room that I had inhabited for so long? Freedom of speech was a thing that I had dreamt of since I was fifteen. Now, at the grand old age of seventeen, I had found my freedom and I wasn't letting go of it.

My first task was to write a letter to my friends and family who had been praying for some form of healing. I felt I owed them a message, an explanation for my silence, and a sort of love letter to them all, each and every person who had thought of me and supported me. It began terribly slowly, but it began.

Dear Bug,

We meet again! The return of Bug! It sounds positively joyful! I am now reaching you in a physical way, by just talking to you. The strangest things happen when you are unable to speak. Thankfully, now that is not the case. I'm getting less and less physiotherapy though; I am just wasting away in bed and they don't seem to be doing anything about it. Well, it's a bit hard when my physiotherapist is the head of the team. There is no one to go to as such. I've spoken the letter to my friends and family and hope that it is well received. You are now going to be my memory, my friend, and my all.

Dear Bug,

Every person here is surprised by how little help I receive from the professionals; it is very hit-and-miss. I try working on my own, willing my body to move, even slightly. There are things called neurological pathways. The more you think through the motions of moving an arm, the more your brain thinks that it has actually done it, just by thinking it through. Pretty cool stuff, eh? This is very tiring though, as it takes up all my brain power and I have very little of that anyway!

Dear Bug,

I decided to sit the professionals down and talk to them about what they were doing. My heart was hammering as I get pretty nervous now since all my dealings with Boss Man. Nevertheless, I've spoken to them.

Firstly, I attacked the physiotherapist, Tall. Because I am ever so passionate about getting better, I tend to get quite feisty, to say the least.

"I don't understand why you leave me untreated. Please explain this to me because really I do want to understand. I have a body that is stiffening up and is at risk of contracting and no one is even doing passive movements with me." I passionately pushed for an answer but he remained silent.

"Please tell me there is some reason. I watch every other person get physiotherapy every day or at least three times a week and I am lucky if I get one session, yet I am the most disabled here!"

Nothing.

"I don't want to be lying in a bed for the rest of my life! I want to be able to sit in a chair and I want to be walking. I shouldn't have to *ask* for physiotherapy. You know I'm too ill and that is why I need your help. Help me! Please!" I said in exasperation.

"I. . . I will do my best. I'm sorry," he responded feebly.

I now get physiotherapy regularly, to stretch my limbs. Result!

Dear Bug,

Whilst one area of my care has started to improve, the other has only worsened: I am now getting little, if any, occupational health visits. I assumed that the same approach would work there but I was very wrong indeed! I explained how I felt and what I wanted to be doing and this turned into a heated argument.

"Are you telling me that I'm not doing my job properly?"

My occupational therapist (OT) raised her voice, so out of character with her usual kindly ways that I was shocked.

I thought about her accusation. Well, yes, really that is what I'm saying! One session a week when others are getting four seems a little bit unfair, especially when I am starting to make some significant improvements.

"Are you?" she repeated.

"Not really, I'm just asking how often you are meant to come and see me?" I replied.

Not much was said after that.

Dear Bug,

I did something a little bit naughty today and recorded when somebody was speaking to me. I was trying you out and didn't realise I had pressed record. The student nurse shouted at me and the ward manager was brought in because I had recorded her. It startled me somewhat and I vowed never to do it again. Ever.

CHAPTER TWENTY-THREE

Horror Story

Maria, who took Holly's place on the ward, was a manic depressive. I knew it even if the team looking after her didn't want to admit it. She had more things mentally wrong with her than I did physically and that was a lot. She was nice all the same and treated me in a motherly way.

I explained what had happened with Jackson and she asked me to tell her what he looked like. I did and she went off for a walk.

"I've seen him," she said in shock. "He's outside talking to Clive."

"No way!" I exclaimed.

To be honest, I didn't really believe her because he wasn't allowed on the ward. I had an agitated night's sleep but I couldn't work out why. One bad night turned into two nights and I was left slightly bemused by my interrupted sleep patterns.

I told Maria about my restless nights in a conversational way, whilst she ate her breakfast.

"I know you haven't been sleeping," she said quietly, with concern in her voice. I did a double take. "Before you ask me how I know, you were screaming in the night and saying his name. I tried to see if you were okay."

I was stunned, even in a hospital that was normally so loud, the silence was so intense that you could probably have heard a pin drop. It was broken by the old lady in the bed next door to me.

"Did somebody say screaming? Yes, you were screaming and shouting in the night. Everything alright?"

"Yes," I said defiantly and hastily added, "Thank you." She carried on eating.

"I think, although you believe yourself to be over this, Jess, the mere mention that I saw him has set your subconscious brain into override. You are not over it and the sooner you realise that the better."

Her words stung, but I probably needed that.

Maybe I should ask for help, I pondered. *I need to do something because it's just embarrassing having no control over what I'm saying at night.*

The counsellor came around later that day and I braced myself before I began.

"I need to ask for some help please. I've been thinking about what happened with Jackson lately and I need to talk about it."

"You won't be talking about it here."

As if I had said something dirty.

"But don't you see? I need to talk about it," I said in mild confusion as I tried to get through to her.

"Not here." And she changed the subject.

There was absolutely no one I could speak to.

*

Mornings were routine, I would ask who was on the day shift

before I had my breakfast, just so I knew. On one morning, it was a carer who was known as 'Sick Note' that came to open my curtain at some godforsaken time in the morning.

Her appearance was unusual because she had been off forever with various problems. The other nurses thought she was taking the piss, which made her unpopular.

Due to her absence, she hadn't been working since the abuse had surfaced. I asked her my usual daily question.

"Who's on today please?"

"Err. . . Leyla, Louise, Carl, Jackson. . ."

"What? Jackson?" I interrupted her, my heart pounding. "There isn't a Jackson who works on this ward."

"Yes, there is Jess. You remember—small, Asian guy."

"No. Please, no. Christ! No, help me! You don't understand," I stumbled over my words as the shock engulfed me.

Panic-stricken tears streamed down my face like a fast-flowing river. I tried to form words but I was shaking hysterically now.

Why was he back? How? Where? What was I going to do?

"But I love you, Jess." His voice came swimming into my mind.

How could this have happened? I had been in The Promised Land for eighteen months by this time. Now the man who verbally and sexually abused me for five months was working on the same ward as I was in. I didn't know what to do. I asked for my phone and just about pressed the button with my working finger to send a text.

Shit! He's back working. Help me.

I sent it to Mum, Dad, Tom and another family friend. Frenzies of messages came through, all trying to hide their fear, whilst I shook uncontrollably. There was outrage and a fierce protective response from everyone. Dad wanted to ring the ward and so did Tom, who never liked to speak to people on the phone. Mum wanted to come straight up to the hospital to be with me.

The nurse appeared—a big African woman strolled towards me.

"Do not let any man scare you this much. Let God bring him punishment. God is who should judge. You are a strong woman; you have so much more to offer. Don't let any man take that away from you," she said, almost shouting it with the passion in her voice.

The ward manager came. He had betrayed me. I continued to shake and freeze alternately with fear.

"It doesn't mean we don't believe you, Jess. He's only just come back—it's been six months since it happened. Why is it such a problem?" he questioned.

"Why? You promised me that he would never be on this ward whilst I remained on it. You lied and I trusted you."

Soon, Dad had thoroughly sorted out the ward manager who was now pitifully scared of him. Dad had kept every email that passed between him and the ward manager and there was clear, written evidence of the agreement that whilst I was on the ward Jackson would not work there.

I was shamed and looked at like I was dirty. Did he have this problem? I imagined not. No, justice had failed me. I was the victim, yet I was being treated like the culprit, the traitor, punished even. I was the one who had upset the 'harmony' on the ward.

The male staff did not come near me for I reeked of danger. I was toxic to them. I didn't feel like 'Jess' anymore. I had grown out of the name. I felt as if I was an outsider in a place I didn't know anymore. Everyone called me Jess, and I didn't want that. That's what Jackson called me. I couldn't trust him. The ward manager called me that. He had betrayed me by letting the bastard back on the ward whilst I was still there.

I wanted a fresh start, so from now on I wanted to be called by my full name. Jessica would not be treated like the proverbial. Jessica wouldn't stand for that. She was the person I would grow into.

There was a Christian carer with whom I got on quite well. She was an interesting character, someone who enjoyed a heated debate. Her religious views were strict, yet caring at the same time. I always imagined that she lived by the phrase, 'What would Jesus do?'

We got along well. Her children were much older than me and she was much older than my mum. I suppose it shows that age is only a number. I had thought we understood one another and respected each other's opinions even if they weren't similar.

"You know you should forgive him," she said flatly. "Whatever went on."

I looked at her and replied, "Oh, should I? I think maybe if you had gone through what I did you might think differently."

"Maybe it was a lesson of some sort. For him or for you. You should forgive him."

A lesson? I thought silently. *A lesson?* I was astounded and infuriated by her words as once again my heart shattered into a million pieces.

Jackson had won. He walked free. Maybe if it had been her child she would have thought differently, but it wasn't her child. The dirty secret was my family's burden.

I felt unable to talk to anybody else about Jackson after that, let alone those who actually cared for me, for fear of getting the same kind of response.

Although keeping quiet was easier, I promised myself that, one day, the real story would find its way to the surface. I would write a book and I would tell the truth. I would tell it when I was ready. Maybe I was extremely poorly but I would get better, eventually. He had picked the wrong woman this time.

Vulnerable I may be but I was born a fighter, and this will only temporarily break me, I told myself firmly.

The agony of the M.E. Monster infiltrated my body and tortured me from the inside. Exhaustion seeped through me until there was silence. My limbs felt as heavy as rocks. I desperately tried to fight it, holding onto the dream of freedom.

I took my mind to the beauty of Bluebell Hill where the trees danced a slow waltz with one another and the sun kissed my cheeks but did not hurt. There, I could rest blissfully on green banks as life went on around me. I could rest and think. Gran's voice became a part of my peaceful vision.

"Yes, my darling, rest. We will write a book together, just you and me, Jess sweetheart, I promise it will happen."

I would write a book and justice would be done. He wouldn't win—I couldn't let him. I would have the last say.

CHAPTER TWENTY-FOUR

Escape to Narnia

In order to escape The Promised Land, I had to speak to numerous psychiatrists and psychologists, trying desperately to convince them that my illness was not just in my head.

Lots of visitors came from all over Kent, as they tried to find a suitable place for me to go to, now The Promised Land had apparently tried their best.

"No, I don't want to be ill!" I shouted at the many psychologists and psychiatrists who came to test me, because speaking calmly in clear English didn't seem to translate properly to their blinkered views.

It was difficult because I hadn't made the miraculous recovery they had been promised and walked out miles better, to them it must be something that I was or wasn't doing.

Now, it was back to more people like Psycho Woman, to decide what had caused my lack of progress. They looked at me like I was thick, inferring I had willed this debilitating illness onto myself. I mean, who believes this shit? Honestly?

I had a whole life that I loved, which I had to leave behind because the M.E. Monster had taken control of every aspect of my life.

I tried to be nice to them. I tried so damn hard to but it was clear that they had already made decisions about me before even meeting me. I was already labelled damaged goods to them.

It's just water off a duck's back. Stay calm, I had thought with all my willpower.

But they claimed that I had chosen this. Chosen to make up this ludicrous story about being severely ill, because that conclusion justified the cheaper option of locking me away in an unknown place, rather than treating me as an individual who needed help.

I was poorly, very poorly at that. I couldn't move and I couldn't get them to move out of my personal space. Did every person with M.E. have to fight against this unbearable gag in order to get better?

Nowhere would take me. All the places that were suggested were 'not equipped to deal with such a complex case.'

There were several meetings in which doctors came from afar to see me, yet there was little success. I was trying to keep my sanity together.

Finally, a medical doctor came and saved me.

"Tell me what to do!" I cried. "Please tell me what to do and I'll do it. I'm just. . . too tired." I grimaced with the pain of every breath.

It was like there was a boulder in my way, stopping me from passing. Stabbing nerve pains riddled my aching body. He asked me so many questions, from what the name of my cat at home was to what I ate for breakfast. Everything under the sun. He then came to a conclusion.

"I don't think that Neuro-rehab would work for you because it is too high pace. We expect you to go home after a month."

He looked up at my crestfallen face. This had been the last possible place that would take me on.

"But, there is a place I know that is for people with M.E. and all sorts of conditions, which works on much slower progress level, particularly holistic care. They are not expecting results quickly like this place does. I will see what I can do."

This had been a God send. The stress of all the interviews over the past few months had taken their toll. Not long after this medical doctor had visited (I hadn't even caught his name), my parents came to visit and told me that he had called them to talk through his plan.

This was the first time that a doctor had involved my parents before deciding plans since Sunshine Ward, nearly two years ago. They sounded positive that they had been asked their opinion too.

A week later, another doctor and a counsellor came to see me from the new hospital. It really was my last chance. However, there was something different about these two professionals; they were kind, the doctor held my hand and they talked to me in whispers, knowing that I was sound sensitive. They truly understood, which was a blessed relief.

"It's okay, love. We are going to take you to a new hospital. It's only small in comparison to this but we shall sort your pain out and get you some physiotherapy that isn't Graded Exercise. I'm not sure I believe that will work."

I sighed with relief as exhilaration filled my aching bones.

"Where?" I managed to gasp.

"It's called Narnia and it is in Kent. There is a lake and fields surrounding us and in the snow it is just beautiful, but we shall let you decide, Jessica. One thing that I can promise is that it is quieter than here, much quieter. I will ring your family, I want them to know that you will be safe with us. It would be nice if they could visit too, just to make sure they are happy."

Again, I sighed with relief as exhilaration filled my bones. The only downside was that I would have to wait until after Christmas to go there.

I had wanted out of The Promised Land for so long, I didn't belong and just as I found a place where maybe I could, I would have to wait another two months to get there.

I sobbed to Mum and Dad when I found out that I would have to wait to get to Narnia.

*

I was hurtling along the motorway in another ambulance that sounded like it was talking to me. This time I was hurtling away from The Promised Land, away from Boss Man, away from Jackson, and all the staring carers too.

I had gone into The Promised Land as an innocent child; I had left a deeply scarred young woman, far older than my seventeen years. As I breathed in the calming Entonox to try to numb the sounds of the roads and the effect of the motion, I couldn't help but feel a little exhilaration of freedom. I had escaped! I had finally escaped the hellish place that I had lived in for eighteen months.

Thinking of all the battles I had fought, finding my way to this hidden Narnia was the culmination of my victories. I knew it was going to be something pretty special. Then again, I had thought The Promised Land would be something incredible and it had turned out to be hell on earth.

As if he had heard my last thoughts, Dad squeezed my hand and smiled.

"Won't be long now, sweetheart."

I had met countless people during my fight against the M.E. Monster who claimed to be professionals'but I had learned to use the term most lightly. There had been doctors, psychologists and neurologists.

It had taken Narnia six months to find me. Six months out of my twenty-one month stay is how long it had been since The Promised Land had decided they wanted me out. The time that coincided, coincidentally, with my speaking out about Jackson.

Obviously, it was easier to get rid of me than deal with the problem in hand because what had happened to me made them look really bad. Nobody would want to send their vulnerable loved ones to a place where they would be in danger of abuse, not if they knew about it beforehand.

Mum had described her visit to Narnia as "beautiful" and "just the right place for her Jessica," but no one could have prepared me for the reality.

The ambulance entered Narnia's grounds and Dad looked out of the window at the endless beauty that met his eye. Both Mum and Dad were finally happy that I would be nearer to them and in a place that seemed so much friendlier.

The program was better too. They worked with the person to make the best possible outcome. My parents had seen this on their visit and had met the doctor, who had put them at peace.

"You know, Jessica, if I were ever ill, this would be the place to bring me. It is just a wonderful place. . . and the view!" Dad smiled broadly. "It's just a bugger to get an ambulance to!" he added as we hopped over a speed bump in the road.

I had met many interesting folk along my journey at The Promised Land but I was very glad that I was now starting a new chapter. I had officially passed the title of 'CFS Granny' (it had been my title for over a year) to somebody else!

The last few steps of this part of the climb to recovery were tough. My exhausted body had been hit from all angles and really struggled to climb those last steps.

I continued to breathe in the Entonox to keep the sound of the ambulance muffled. I felt it stop. We had arrived. So much talk of what might be was now focused on this moment.

I lay on the ambulance trolley as it rattled over the gravel and breathed in the cool, fresh air whilst the anticipation grew to fever pitch. I was inside the eccentric building and people were going out of their way to be welcoming, wishing me well as I passed.

I reached the room called Wisteria and, before long, using a pat slide, was moved from the trolley onto a warm comfy bed. The Entonox would soon put me into a hazy rest but not before the carer had popped in to introduce herself.

Diana was a lady with a personality that was larger than life and she hurried over to whisper, "Hello! Welcome to Narnia, let me unpack your things."

I nodded my appreciation and whispered back, "Thanks." It was all I could do for now. I was too exhausted.

This is crazy, I thought, *people actually wanting to help me?*

I couldn't say that there had been nobody at The Promised Land who cared for me; there were some really nice people (mixed with some rather rotten ones too). But this place felt different.

Even before I had said my goodbyes, any concerns and

worries I had from my time at The Promised Land had been shrugged off my shoulders.

The only shock to my system on that first day in Narnia was when I was left alone. I had nobody to talk to as there was no bay; I was isolated to just one room. Yet, when I buzzed for help with brushing my teeth, there was no, "Oh, for fuck's sake," from the nurses, instead they were keen to help and had no problem brushing my teeth.

The biggest change came with my first meal. I had initially lost tons of weight from not having the energy or physical ability to eat properly. Once they got the NG tube down me, my weight went back up. I had never been big but being fed the right nutrients had made me become a size ten rather than my usual size eight. Big for me, but still a long way from fat.

Then when the NG tube was removed, I dramatically dropped ten kilos, which was a lot to lose on my small, fragile frame.

The food had never been a strength at The Promised Land but they at least tried. I would eat everything even though it was tasteless because I was desperate to put some weight onto my diminished size zero frame.

In Narnia, it couldn't have been more different. I looked at my first meal with wonder and the first mouthful I was fed had me jumping for joy inside my head.

"Oh, my goodness!" I exclaimed. "It actually tastes like beef!"

With each mouthful, I couldn't stop grinning broadly at the taste of the food. Who cared if it was puréed? It tasted amazing.

"Oh wow! It really is such a pleasure to feed you!" Diana said excitedly with a smile appearing on her face.

There were vegetables that tasted like real vegetables! Not the watery gunk I had become so accustomed to. It was a real joy just to eat. The chef would try to cook me anything I liked. My favourite dish being either salmon on a bed of Mediterranean vegetables or stuffed aubergines. Finally, all the weight I had lost returned, even though I was eating no more than usual.

My little room was fast becoming a home; other people came in and out of it but to me, it became my entire world.

One night, when it was dark, they opened my curtains and I looked out in absolute awe. I could actually see a tree! I got such joy at seeing a tree with a rabbit hopping along underneath it. Real life lay out before me and all I could do was gaze at the beauty of it.

"I haven't seen a tree in years and it's even longer since I've seen a rabbit," I marvelled.

"Then we must make sure you see plenty of them!" The nurse smiled.

In my mind's eye, I allowed the trees to dance in the moonlight, whilst the stars twinkled in the dusk. It was the first time I had seen the sky in such a long time.

The clouds that momentarily blocked my view of the stars moved to a rhythm because the Earth thrums to a unique beat as it spins on its axel—one that can never be heard but always seen.

CHAPTER TWENTY-FIVE

The Love Letter

Dear Bug,

My dream of sitting out of bed in a chair on my eighteenth birthday means everything to me. I have worked endlessly to try and make it happen. I would give the world for it. Too many other dreams have gone zooming out of the window— I'm not going to let that be the case this time. This is the big one-eight! It seemed like I was fifteen just a few moments ago. Where have the years gone?

My sweet sixteen had been spent with a few helium balloons around my bed. It wasn't meant to have been like that. It's fair to say that I'm not living the normal life of a seventeen-year-old preparing for the big one-eight. This isn't by choice. If choice had anything to do with my life, it would be an incredibly different tale but going out celebrating with massive parties isn't even a consideration, as it would be impossible.

Birthdays are different when you are chronically unwell. They are either a great reminder of what I don't have or just another milestone that I have to watch pass through my fingers. They serve as a reflection of what is now important in my life. It's not boyfriends or late nights out that make my memories.

Instead, it is the moment I managed to move a finger, or speak, achieving visible progress. These are the things that form my memories now.

I won't lie, there is a big part of me that yearns for a normal life but I can't dwell on that because that lifestyle no longer represents who I am. Times change.

But, my God, this bed hurts me to just lie still. I turn any frustrations at the daily horror I am facing into my dream to sit out in a chair. I have tried to make each birthday count in some way. Memories can never be remade so it is important to make each moment special.

At The Promised Land, they told me that sitting in a chair was an attainable goal so I have put everything into achieving that one dream. What would it feel like to be actually sitting up? These sorts of questions drive me forwards, strengthening my resolve to try and achieve it. I want it so much. It is my every thought.

I believe with every breath that I will make it happen. This meant more passive movements with the physiotherapist and getting used to being at a more elevated position for food. Trying to get used to all this when my body was so stiff, was difficult. I had to have the physical energy to be able to try this mammoth task, let alone the mental energy too.

The exhaustion from my efforts has been such that at the moment, I can't even bear visitors. My family come and go, their words not really making any sense in my mind. I only have the energy to see them once a week; my heart cries for them but I have to get better. There is no alternative way of achieving my goal.

Every time Becky walks in and shuts that door to the rest

of the world, I hold onto the thought of the chair and being with her on my birthday.

Becky is growing up, looking even more like my beautiful mum and so very stylish. My family couldn't be more dedicated to my recovery but the hardest knock came when I was told that I would have to stop seeing my friends if I wanted to achieve my goal.

The lack of energy meant I could either try to sit in a chair for my birthday or see some of my friends. Not both. Just one.

Dr Nice laid it out for me so gently, "It's your choice. Which means more to you?"

My friends will understand, won't they? I wanted to follow my heart but it was being pulled in two different directions. What could I do, Bug? I don't want to live the rest of my life like this—lying on my back in a bed, unable to move. I have to have some part of my fairy tale ending come true! I will only be eighteen once and I am determined that it will mark the turn in this wretched condition. . . so I chose.

Being on my own all the time, even in a loving environment, was not easy. In my reverie, I climbed mountains; I walked into the sunlight with the sun kissing my cheeks. The grass tickled my head as I lay on the warm ground, laughing with my friends. Nick laughed with me. There was complete harmony as we ran, carefree, and playing like kids do. Such simple dreams but it was all I wanted. That was what I was fighting for.

My body was virtually paralysed from the neck down. This had been exacerbated by the exhaustion from moving hospitals. My arms did not move thanks to the heavy braces that I had been wearing for well over a year now. When the physiotherapists came, they had to heave my pain-ridden body in order to move me passively. It was such desperately hard work that they would often fumble.

My arms were in a form of contraction again, this time they were stuck straight due to my elbow tendons and ligaments being so stiff. The sheer agony I had faced previously came back to bite me. I was fighting round two thanks to the lack of physiotherapy at The Promised Land.

"Ready Jessica? We shall do it together," the physiotherapist said.

"On my count. . . one. . . two. . . three. . . GO!" I said in response.

I yelped. I groaned. I moaned. Pain. Agony. *Help!* Then I felt like an athlete, Wonder Woman in the making, as I focused on being in the zone.

In my mind, I completely blocked out the agony. I told myself that there was no pain; I could feel the fluidity in my elbow as it bent further than it had the day before. The stiffness melted like candle wax. In reality, sheer, searing pain made my insides squirm and my eyes water. It took every bit of my inner strength to hold it together but giving up was not an option.

After a few moments, we stopped and prepared to do it all again.

I want arms that can move and don't get stuck at ninety degrees, I told myself.

So, I did it again and again until I couldn't physically do it anymore. Then we stopped for the day, ready to start again in the morning. This was not Graded Exercise Therapy which was where the exercise was upped by a percentage every week. Instead, it was completely necessary movement—without it I would not be able to move at all and I simply couldn't let that happen.

Despite having moved back to my home county, where I was closer to my friends, I had never felt so alone. No matter how close they were geographically, they remained so far away from me because of the isolation necessary for my big birthday dream to happen. I hoped they would understand; I hoped they knew I was doing it for a better tomorrow.

I needed to get better and I was sacrificing everything to achieve that goal. In my heart of hearts, I couldn't just leave it with me being silent. It didn't feel right. I decided to write a love letter to them all, dictating the words, one by one, so that my one-to-one carer could type it. A letter from the heart that would explain everything.

To my dearest friends,

I want to thank you so much for sticking by my side through everything that has gone on. I am so grateful for your unconditional love and feel so lucky to have you all. I am preparing to try and sit in a chair for my birthday. This task means everything to me and is my most ambitious task yet. Sadly, the only way this will be possible is if I don't have any visitors before my birthday. My doctor has limited me to just my close family but I promise that, when the day does come when you can visit, you will see me as a much better me and further along the road to recovery.

God bless you and know that I love you greatly,
Jessica

I hoped it didn't sound too sickly. I would have to wait until Sunday, when I would be seeing Mum, before I sent it.

Over night, I became acutely unwell, hot and cold, with a raging temperature and my eyes felt like they were bulging out of their sockets. I lost my speech within an instant. It turned out that I had come down with a virus that my body wasn't able to fight. All of my plans seemed to be falling apart at my feet.

A few days of doing nothing, with no visitors, I will recover, I reassured myself, *and everything will be okay*.

The doctors were concerned for my frail body that was not fighting the virus because my immune system was so low.

This would happen three weeks before my birthday! Come on body, fight!

There was a knock at the door and my carer came in whispering urgently, "Your friends are here from school. They are demanding they see you."

My heart sank but I was too weak to speak. Half of me wanted it so badly, just to see the familiar faces of those who I loved, but the other half was focused on a dream that I was told would be less achievable if I had extra visitors.

You would imagine that having visitors when you are chronically ill is something to be excited about. But the reality for somebody with severe M.E. is that it causes all the symptoms to flare up.

I didn't know how to code to the carer that this was not okay. It wasn't meant to be like this! I had planned the moment when I was going to see my friends again. We were going to laugh and chat like normal teenagers should and I would be sitting in that beautiful chair.

The M.E. Monster wasn't considerate enough to allow me to

have that moment. It didn't care about how my friends would react to walking into the room to no response from their friend who was too ill to even think. I heard them come in.

Suddenly, a blotchy rash covered my body, whilst they stood watching me. The carer had left for a brief moment to let me, "have some time with my friends." I was boiling but freezing all at once. My brain felt like it was swelling, as I tried to take in how much each of the four had changed in such a short space of time.

I was exhausted before their first word was whispered. They just stared at me like I was an exhibit in a museum, not knowing what to do. All the while, the M.E. Monster tortured me.

We were living in different worlds. They didn't understand mine and I couldn't understand theirs. One thing was certain, my friends were giving up on me. They had been in my life since I was twelve but now their faces were vacant. There was no more I could do to change this. I gathered all of my energy and whispered, "I love you, thank you." But I don't think they could understand my words.

The M.E. Monster continued to torture me for days as punishment for my efforts. I wish they could have seen this ongoing battle I fought and not just the exhibit lying still and sick on a bed on their brief visit.

Why did they have to come uninvited? Of course, I loved the girls. I would always love the girls, but the payback was chronic, especially because the virus had already made me so incredibly poorly.

Everything I had worked for was gone in a flash. The floor had been taken out from underneath me and I was left with nothing.

The chair didn't happen and the letter was never sent. Instead, I spent my eighteenth birthday living it large in bed. My carer put my makeup on and I was dressed in a prom dress as I would have if the M.E. Monster wasn't sucking the life out of me. My hair was made over too, lying in soft curls on my pillow.

I spent the day with those closest to me being in the room for just moments at a time. Nick was there for a fleeting time, for his birthday was the day before mine. Mum, Becky and Dad were all there for short parts of the day.

The dream had shattered into a million pieces. My birthday came and went and I was still unable to hold much of a conversation. Maybe it just wasn't meant to be. Maybe it wouldn't have happened anyway but hanging over me was the thought that if the girls hadn't visited, if I had done as the doctor said, would I be sitting in that beautiful chair that I had longed for with all of my heart?

CHAPTER TWENTY-SIX

Remembering Easter

Good Friday

Being in a Christian hospital meant that Easter celebrations were quite prominent. I usually found these celebrations to be quite an enjoyable affair but this time was to be different.

It was Good Friday. The day before I had been feeling quite emotional. I wanted Dad to just make things better and move me home. That's what I wanted most of all.

I wanted to go home. Sometimes I got that overwhelming urge to be free in the arms of Becky, Tom and Mum because living in hospital is not easy.

I didn't spend a huge amount of time thinking like this, thinking of what I wished I had, because the simple matter was I couldn't have it. I could only have it by getting better, so that is what I focused on. Time is an endless entity; you could start thinking about it and get no further.

I had woken up feeling even more sick than the day before. I hadn't fully recovered from before my birthday, but this felt different. A massive burning rash would appear and disappear within moments. My temperature had gone up and I couldn't place what was wrong. Nevertheless, I tried to carry on even though my body really didn't like it and I would lay in agony.

When it came to food time, I managed a few mouthfuls before I was sick, very sick.

Squeak, the carer with a squeaky voice, was only a tiny lady but she managed to roll me onto my side quickly just before I was sick again. Then I was out.

I interviewed a carer on the shift named Diana, who had made notes on what had happened to me when I blacked out.

Notes from Diana

Jessica was turned onto her side, at which point her eyes rolled to the back of her head and she began vigorously convulsing. She nearly fell off the bed but I held her tightly with the help of Squeak. When the convulsing didn't stop, we shouted for help because the alert button wasn't working and we finally managed to get Dr Nice.

"Woah, woah, Jessica, what are you up to? Alright love," he said soothingly, as he held onto Jessica.

It wasn't really rigors because her temperature was only 37.8 but she was fitting with no end in sight.

"Come on Jessica, you are going to wear yourself out!" Dr Nice said.

Squeak and I continued to talk quietly, telling Jessica that it was okay and she was perfectly safe.

Come on, I thought desperately, you need to pull through this now.

It was decided to give rectal diazepam. My aim was to stay there until everything settled but it was hard work. I couldn't begin to imagine how exhausting it must be for our Sunshine. The rectal diazepam seemed to slowly work, thank God. Her very tired body flopped.

They decided to put her on a constant anti-emetic through a syringe drive. Although I did not want to leave her, the care work I had to do elsewhere was building up—it had taken over an hour to stop the seizure.

I decided that I would keep going back to visit her. It pained me to leave her sickly pale face but her one-to-one would be there soon. I just needed a drink of some sort. Jessica looked settled enough for me to go. I needed some air to think about what was happening to our little ray of light.

Diana x

*

I found myself in a daze; the song 'Fields of Gold' was playing on repeat in my head but I didn't know why. There were a lot of things I didn't know right then but I was too exhausted to even try to find some explanation. Comforting voices were telling me that I had done really well but my limbs were telling me otherwise. It felt like they had moved more today than ever before. The pain in my stomach was increasing and I was sick again. Two hours passed and then. . .

*

Notes from Diana
I could hear my name being called and I hurried in that direction.

"Diana! Diana! Jessica's room!" a voice called.

As soon as I got to the doorway, I could see that her eyes were rolled backwards and she was convulsing violently again. I rushed to help but this time was different from the last. Her breathing was shallow, yes, but now it was slow and calm.

"Jessica, my darling, I am here, it's alright, honey."

I felt quite stupid just talking, trying to think of what to say but there wasn't much time to think and I thought it would be calming to hear a voice that you knew well.

Dr Nice arrived shortly after me and surveyed the situation.

"Oh Jessica, you are making me grow even more grey!"

There was some nervous laughter before he started to assess her.

"There is no panic in her breathing. Why is this happening? We've got to put a stop to these convulsions. How do we do this?"

He mused over different ideas before coming up with a plan.

"Rectal diazepam 10mg should work for more than two hours, I mean it really should. I think another dose of diazepam and then, once we've stopped it, we can have another think. But my immediate instinct is to add some midazolam to the syringe drive and sedate her until we can get this under control.* The next few days are crucial."

We all agreed and, after a few minutes of bustling around, the diazepam had been given and the syringe drive changed. I could only hope for the best as I left.

Diana x

(*Midazolam is a sedative and diazepam is a strong muscle relaxant for those of you who don't know.)

*

After the hours of chaos, it was blissful to have some silence. My arms and legs felt like they had run a marathon and the stabbing pain in my stomach was agony. I didn't really know what was going on, only that I felt rough as hell.

A few hours passed in which I felt like I was being slowly cast under a spell of exhaustion. I wasn't here and I wasn't there; I drifted in a draining dream-like place. It was as if I was in a trance. I could no longer utter a word and my mind was fuzzy and strange but I couldn't locate the reason for it.

I was told that I needed to have some gabapentin (an epilepsy drug that was normally used for my nerve pain) but the rest of my meds could be missed. I can remember that part; everything else that was just a blizzard of information that I did not care much for. Feeling so sick all the time made it hard to swallow even the tiniest bit of water. I was looking forward to sleep.

*

Easter Saturday
Exhausted. . . stabbing pain in my tummy. . . completely exhausted. . . sip water. . . sip more. . . confusion as to why I felt like this. . . weak. One-to-one came. . . she was shocked at the difference from when she last saw me. . . but I was tired. . . with a head-thumping hangover but without the alcohol. . . I want Mum. . . I want Diana. . . but no speech. . . it hurt to think, so I didn't. . . They kept putting water in. . . but

felt sick. . . I was tired. . . just tired. . . ouch. . . I hurt. . . The pain was everywhere. . . so confused as to why. . . sipping water. . . Mum's voice. . . Dad's too. . . that's better. . . Mum and Dad.

"My baby, what's wrong with my baby?"

My ghostly white pallor had shocked my mum. I didn't look like her Jessie baby. *What the hell had happened?* Her thoughts could be read like an open book.

"Why weren't we called?" she whispered and exchanged concerned looks with Dad. "Baby, what has happened?"

She desperately tried to make sense of the situation. Why hadn't they called Mum or Dad? Becky was kept out of the room: it was hard enough for my parents to see me drugged up, let alone my thirteen-year-old sister. They decorated my room with Easter eggs and fluffy little chickens—all plastic because I couldn't eat dairy or egg.

Dr Nice came in to explain the situation. I don't really know what he said as the words wriggled into one another and made no sense but, my goodness, my tummy hurt. The only word I heard was "stable." That must be good news; I must be getting better.

"Want a sip baby?" Mum whispered, as she stroked my hair.

Exhaustion seeped through every vein like a drug, as shooting pains ran up my arms and legs, electrifying me. I fell into a dazed sleep just to rest my eyes that little bit more becasue they hurt too.

The night staff came on and were visibly concerned. The day had passed with little less than a quarter of a cup of water and it was beginning to show. I was grey, not passing urine, and looked a shadow of myself.

They nursed me through the night but were getting more and more worried, as my observations showed my pulse and temperature were high, but my blood pressure was incredibly low. I was oblivious to this. I hoped tomorrow I would be better.

*

Easter Sunday
But I wasn't better. In fact, I was much worse. The dehydration was visible in my dull eyes. I was pain-ridden and drugged. My speech hadn't come back, my body was a sickly greyish yellow and I was very weak, painfully so. Nobody could get the doctor to listen to their pleas.

"She needs a hospital with an emergency department," they pleaded.

Dr Nice said he would try one more thing. "Her M.E. won't cope with the journey," he said in way of explanation for not heeding their pleas.

The night nurse cried, at a loss for what to do. I tried to perk up, I tried to push to the surface, but I kept falling. I thought of my lovely gran and imagined her by my side. Her soft touch on my tummy soothed the pain; she wiped away any fear of what was happening. I could never be scared with my gran by my side and, anyway, I was too damn exhausted.

Today was Easter Sunday, the day Christ returned from death. Everything was going to be okay. I was glad Mum and Dad weren't here today; I didn't want them to worry.

Dr Nice entered the room with a nurse.

"Okay Jessica, we are going to have to put in a NG tube. This is only a temporary measure, just until we get you back to where you were love. Don't see this as a step backwards," he whispered in a jolly fashion.

I wasn't able to tell anyone about my tummy; maybe they could tell it wasn't right.

The tube was passed and went in relatively pain-free. I realised how much I did not miss those bloody tubes. The Fortijuice (fruits of the forest flavour) was pushed down manually every ten minutes. Fortijuice is a build-up drink full of all the goodness you needed to put on weight. It is also incredibly rich and sickly. My God, I had never felt so sick but I tried to keep it down, even though the pain in my stomach had reached fever pitch.

So far, they had been pushing it down slowly through the tube but it only took one nurse to ruin it. This nurse pushed it in too quickly and it felt like she had stabbed me in the stomach with a knife. I couldn't tell you exactly where the pain was coming from but tears poured down my face as she left the room. Then I was sick and sick and sick. Diana came in answer to my moans of discomfort.

"Alright sweetie, it's alright," she said softly.

Someone came to join her and help clean me up. Then I was violently sick and the tube that was supposed to be up my nose and down into my stomach was hanging out of my mouth. The room stank of fruits of the forest as they pressed the emergency button but nobody came.

"H. . . hel. . . hel. . . p," I groaned.

To the despair of Dr Nice, there was no option but to go to hospital. His main concern was for what he knew the journey would do to my M.E., but I don't think he realised quite how unwell I was.

My family were called and they were soon hurtling down the motorway to be by my side. Diana joined me in the ambulance as it moved quickly over the bumps. Every time I was sick, I had to be rolled further onto my side to prevent me from choking.

"There is nothing left in you, honey," she said soothingly and she was right. I felt empty.

At the local hospital, we were hurried through hugely loud sounds and then out into a quieter side room at Dr Nice's request. The sound levels were booming and I could barely understand what was going on. They took bloods and the doctor came.

"Does it hurt here?" he asked. "Here?"

I yelped. Oh good God. It burned—searing agony on my right side, just in from my hip. Then my temperature was taken and it presented at 39.7 degrees.

They rushed around doing many things at the same time but I couldn't understand what they were saying. Mum and Dad arrived. Oh thank God, it was Mum and Dad.

Diana embraced them, saying how grateful she was to see them. She kissed me then disappeared.

The doctor arrived, taking more bloods with painful arterial punches.

"We think it is appendicitis. It could explain her symptoms, or a twisted ovary. Once we have her in surgery we shall sort everything. The plan is to take her now. Thank you for your time."

He left instantly. I was changed into a hospital gown and

they failed an attempt to insert a catheter (they eventually succeeded once I was under anaesthetic) before I was hurtling down the corridors with Dad holding my hand amongst the accompanying rows of the surgical team.

"Breathe this oxygen in and I'm just going to press on your neck. Your dad is still here,'" the anaesthetist said kindly.

I was asleep in no time. When they opened me up, they saw the inflamed appendix. Just as they went to remove it, it burst.

Someone must've been looking after me up there.

CHAPTER TWENTY-SEVEN

The Long and Winding Road

I awoke after the operation, dazed, with a numbing pain. I was in a very loud cubicle that Mum told me was mixed gender. When I say loud, I mean as loud as an orchestra, as loud as the Big Bang going off constantly.

My ear plugs couldn't even cope with the sound decibels and this was in the middle of the night too—when everybody was meant to be sleeping.

The man next door was having his lung suctioned and, at one point, the pot with the contents crashed over with a huge, head-splitting smash. Mum and Dad finally left at three in the morning. They were reluctant to leave me on this ward with my sound sensitivity.

I watched each hour pass on the wall clock, trying to come to terms with the bizarre few days that had passed, yet it almost seemed too much to come to terms with; so much had happened. Before long, I started to realise how many people were in the ward. It was horrific.

The lights, the sound, the movement, all blew my mind; they were so damn intense. The light was everywhere, even though Mum had put my dark glasses on. Noise came from all directions and my brain felt on fire. I hummed inside my head, trying to block out some of the noise, but it was no use.

The trolleys came bundling along and a nurse tried to feed me Weetabix soaked in cow's milk. On the inside, I swore.

No. Stop! Listen to me, I thought desperately.

"Soya," I whispered. She couldn't hear. "Please, soya. . . allergic to cow's milk."

She looked at me quizzically as if I had just spoken a foreign language. "No milk? What do you eat?"

"Soya milk," I said, desperately trying to get through to her. Not only did I feel like I had been punched from the inside, I was having to fight ignorance on the outside too.

She tried to remove my dark glasses but I shook my head until she went away. I was panic-stricken because the room was becoming lighter as dawn approached. I realised I really was helpless and so very alone.

How could I be in the loudest place I had ever experienced, yet feel so shockingly alone? It would have been so easy to lose my sanity.

The nurse came back over to me, bringing a halt to my thoughts.

"Soya milk, huh?" she asked as I vehemently swerved away from the bowl.

"Allergic to milk," I cried, I tried to shout it but, in reality, my words were barely a whisper.

"This is soya milk. I went and got some for you. See?" She showed me the carton and I thanked God. I felt sick but I ate the concoction.

Once she had left, the ticking clock made me feel panicky.

The sound was screaming at me as the papers were delivered and the pandemonium of the doctors' ward rounds began.

Take me back to Narnia, please take me back. I need my mum. You don't understand how much I need her. Each sound is making me shake.

The doctors huddled around my bed. They looked at my wound, which was stopping me from coughing and made me feel like I was constantly winded.

One of the doctors peeled off the dressing without speaking to me. I wasn't the only person with severe M.E. in Britain but I was treated like an alien that they didn't know what to do with.

"Nice," he commented with a smile.

Hang on a minute, what about the pain? Why is it hurting me so much? My questions remained unanswered and they moved on.

Thank God Mum came rushing into my cubicle shortly afterwards. I had never been so pleased to see her.

"Oh baby, it is so loud! You are doing so well, darling. It's okay." She soothed my sensory overloaded head.

Finally, somebody who understood me! It just went to show how much you put your life in other people's hands when you are vulnerable.

We finally returned to Narnia later that day. I immediately felt grateful for the silence and for the darkness of my room—everything was so peaceful and calm.

Dr Nice arrived and it was the most welcome face for me to see, considering the agony I was still in.

"You Wonder Woman! I'm so glad to see you. It's just twenty-four hours later and you are already smiling. It's a miracle. It must have been awfully loud and bright."

Mum and Dad explained the situation. He listened intently

to every word and just having that person to hear our voices without judgement was such a relief. It was a unique approach—one that was very special.

The nurses came up too with big grins on their faces.

"Oh Jessica, my darling Jessica," Diana exclaimed as she held my hand. "You've had the nurses crying, me in a state and you've been the talk of the hospital."

"Crying?" I whispered.

"Yes, crying, and quite a lot of it too. We thought we were going to lose you and then to hear that appendicitis was the cause of all of this."

"Why did you think that you were going to lose me?"

It was only after her explanation of what had happened in the "most stressful Easter of her life" that I began to understand how damn lucky I was to still be alive.

"Fruits of the forest used to be my favourite flavour but now I can't bear the smell of it, not after the amount of it you brought up. What have you done to me?" she joked.

Dear Bug,

At first I couldn't let Becky or Tom see me. I was trying to protect them, you see, especially Becky as, in my eyes, she has seen enough.

Mum surprised me by turning up the very next day after I got back from the hospital rather than following the usual strict pattern of visiting once a week.

It was nice and just what I needed because I was struggling to control the pain that the operation had left behind, let alone drink enough or eat enough due to feeling so very sick.

"You've got to drink, Jessica, otherwise you will end up

being admitted to the hospital again." The words of Dr Nice rang in my ears.

Come on, you can pull through this, I encouraged myself.

That's not even the worst of the problems that I have had to contend with since the operation. I knew that I could pull through the drinking and eating but I am just so embarrassed about the other thing. To even write it down feels like a failure on my part. It makes me cringe.

I have grown accustomed to the loss of my dignity, having had somebody else wash me for many years, but one thing that I have held onto has been my continence, until now. The operation messed up my system, Bug. Not only was I physically scarred on the outside but internally many less visible things happened.

They seemingly hit a nerve in my body when they operated. A nerve responsible for telling me when I need to relieve myself, that nerve no longer does its job properly.

It's heart-breaking for an eighteen-year-old to have to admit that this is the case. All of a sudden, I have been reduced to having just thirty seconds to get onto a bedpan before bursting. Thirty seconds in any hospital is not enough time and so this usually results in an accident. What eighteen-year-old has no control of their bladder for goodness sake? Hopefully it will only be temporary.

I apologise profusely every time that it happens; it is so disheartening. An eighteen-year-old shouldn't be in this position; at this age your continence is something you should be able to take for granted. It is just another thing that the M.E. Monster can tick off as having taken away from me.

Love Jessica x

Dear Bug,

I can't let Becky see me like this, not when everything is so out of control. Her mind is incredibly mature for her age but I can't add any more to the burden I have already placed upon her shoulders.

I won't let M.E. win though, even if the fight kills me. I will not be beaten. My exhausted, pain-ridden body is still a warrior, even at its worst. I remind myself of this and, like a warrior, I rise to the challenge. If I can escape death itself through my fighting spirit, then I can beat this illness; I am sure of it. I have to beat it.

After time plays its part, not only will I have tried everything in my power to get better but I will also have succeeded. There may well be a time to come when I will be able to congratulate myself but first I have to contend with all the associated problems like the increasing fear that set upon the nurses when I couldn't pass urine. The shock of all that has happened is confusing my body, Bug.

My puppeteer, my prison warden, M.E., has trapped me again. It tortures me daily in all areas of my body, laughing uncontrollably at its latest conquest within my body, the most embarrassing one yet.

Sod it. We just had to come up with more inventive ways to get my body to start working again, even if it was just a case of thinking practically. What about using heat to stimulate the bladder to work? It was worth a shot and thank God it worked and I could feel the sudden ease of relief surge through me. We were onto a winner, Bug, you and I together.

Love Jessica x

Once the dressing was removed from my wound, I had to somehow de-sensitise the whole of my stomach. It was still immensely sore. Pierced vitamin E capsules were meant to be good for scarring, so I religiously applied it, at first only being able to lay the capsule gel all over the scar and then, after many months, massaging it into the scar as part of the desensitisation process.

Having come so close to death, I realised that I had a lot of things I wanted to do, despite my incapacities. My dream had been to spread a message of hope to others because I knew how much it was needed. How many pages in a newspaper do you have to flick through before you get a positive, heart-warming story? Too many pages in my humble opinion. This was something I needed to change.

If I could lie here being tortured by the M.E. Monster, yet still remain hopeful of a future beyond this, then every person could benefit from me sharing that hope around.

How many people moan about simple everyday tasks that I would simply love to do? Too much ironing? Give me a working body and I will happily do it for you! It was time to spread the hope using art and a person who couldn't move.

Recovering from this huge setback in my life was going to be an arduous affair, a road that was long and winding, with many ups and downs.

CHAPTER TWENTY-EIGHT

A Laugh-O-Gram

There was so little I was capable of doing that it required meticulous planning, but it was also very much a spur of the moment thing. M.E. was controlling my whole existence.

The exhaustion was not sleepy tiredness; it did not go away with a little rest. The tiredness that comes with M.E. hurts. This kind of tiredness is debilitating. This tiredness makes you feel like you have been in a full-on collision with a double-decker bus. Full to the brim with exhaustion—every single day, and that is on good days.

I was tired of feeling trapped, of being the caterpillar in the chrysalis. I wanted to spread my wings and fly. You don't get a choice in this life: you just have to make the most of what you are given. The truth of the matter was I loved living! I may have lost my identity somewhat to M.E. but I hadn't lost the real me, there was just a stupid dot in between.

I had the idea planned in my mind and now it was time to make this dream come true. As far as I was concerned, I was crap at art. I had given it up as a child, despite getting an A* when I was twelve, and had not looked back since. But now things were different. Art was going to give me a creative voice that I could use for good and to help others. This was my plan and my dream.

I was increasingly aware of the countless times that I had escaped death and so I drew on that feeling of euphoria that I was still here, still alive, even if I was stuck in a world of one room, capable of so little.

That 'little' meant everything and I was highly appreciative of everything that I *could* do, all the functions that I still owned. I had my voice with a bit of movement in the form of shaking and nodding my head. Although I hardly had any movement, I had noticed that when you laugh, it's a very physical thing.

It had given me the idea that grew into the plan. By holding a paintbrush in one of my braced-up hands, all somebody would have to do was make me laugh and, hey presto, there would be a very small shake that would create the laughter lines on a piece of paper.

The previous year, I had decided that this was something I was going to do when I was better but after everything that had happened—why not now?

An ECG measures the beats of your heart on a piece of paper so a Laugh-O-Gram would be a way of measuring your laughter. With this in mind, the first painting was relatively simple in design. I planned that it would be like a reel of ECG paper filled with a mixture of my favourite, vibrant colours.

It was time to put laughter into action. I started with a paintbrush balanced in my hand, the canvas leaning on a pillow so it could be reached. It began with teal then moved on to electric blue to violet to magenta pink to a dash of orange and then to my grand finale—gold, symbolic of hope. My hope for the ending of this journey with a dot in between and the beautiful day when I became free.

Once it was finished, I looked upon it with the eyes of a proud mother. This was something creative that I had achieved on my own, nothing meant more than that. It was called a Laugh-O-Gram.

I was very aware of the influence of my gran in this so I dedicated it to her and hoped she was watching with pride. Everything I had learnt about life was thanks to her and I was proud of her impact on my life.

Pop was so proud, as he was an artist in his own right and taught the subject to others. To have it dedicated to Gran made it better. His loss was still so great but he made the effort to keep going and do things in her name.

To unveil my painting, I was dressed as a stereotypical French artist, with a moustache and beret to match my striped top. In truth, this was just the beginning of my mission to spread hope to everybody and, whilst that picture made the front cover of a magazine newsletter, it wasn't enough to fulfil my ambitious dreams. But it was a damn good start.

Dear Bug,

My body isn't recovering well from the surgery. I have been hit with a dash of peritonitis—poisoning from the pus that spattered me when my appendix burst. That kind of poisoning has to come out some way and it has chosen the worst possible place for a teenager: my face. I know that I have to just keep going as the boils appear on my face. It doesn't matter what we do to try and stop them, they just get worse. I have tried all sorts of fancy products that a nurse has given me, but nothing will work.

Love Jessica x

I carried on with my campaign of hope because, whilst people were still dying from this horrible condition, I simply couldn't stop. It was the only choice I had in life.

Outside my one room, the world had dipped into a massive recession but my message was simple: if you can still walk your child to a park then you have more freedom than people like me.

Reality was harsh and it was making people become so negative. It was my hope to change that by showing people that, if I could create art with a body that could do nothing, it was possible for them to live a positive, more fulfilling life. Maybe my artwork could inspire people to paint or simply to look at their lives differently.

I felt it was my duty to continue with this message of hope. At the same time I would be speaking out about my condition because there were many sufferers like me who had no voice. I hoped to be the voice for the voiceless.

The one-to-one care had stopped and I was being looked after by the staff at Narnia again. My clothes collection was growing, with my aim to have a whole new wardrobe for when I could finally walk.

Now I had Diana, the wonderful carer who did more than care. She was showing me all the things I would have learnt purely by being a healthy teenager.

It was people like her who made a difference, even without meaning to. She turned me from a gangly girl who had never had the opportunity to do all the things that a teenager would normally do as part of growing up into a young woman.

Gok Wan became something of a hero, as she started to teach me about different shapes and styles, taking my fashion sense further on from just a cool t-shirt and jeans.

"This is an 'Apple' figure, Jessica," she said showing me the difference between that and a 'Pear' shape. "But I think you would be more like an 'Hourglass' figure. You are quite tall really. The most important thing is that you learn how to dress your figure."

I was turning into a lady, rather than just a body. I could see all the beautiful things little Becky wore and I understood them, even started to know what they meant. I learned to love fashion and the identity you could find within it.

Meanwhile, the next painting was on its way. This one was based on the idea of a sunset. The abstract painting was awash with a warmth of colour.

I asked people what they thought of it and one of the physiotherapists said, "The beauty of the concept, Jessica, is there will always be a tomorrow. The sun will set but it will always rise."

I thought that this was a nice way of putting it and the name Hope seemed just right. The bubbles of laughter could even be felt on the canvas. I had no idea how powerful the effect would be until people actually saw it and I witnessed human emotion taking over. If this is what art is, then it is actually bloody fantastic!

The last painting in the three was the big one. I had got Mum to buy me the biggest piece of canvas she could find. Bold and vibrant, it would represent the beginning of my story. It would be called *Behind Dark Glasses* and the execution would describe every part of my M.E. state from my point of view. It was an important part of the message that these paintings were created entirely by me.

Since I couldn't paint for myself yet, in the traditional method, other means had to be found. I came up with a new idea. After plastering my face with Vaseline, I applied a thick layer of paint in different colours to represent each of my M.E. profiles. Then the canvas was rolled onto my face to get each side and the middle. My lips were always painted in a beautiful Indian gold, a strong colour to symbolise the power of speech for people in my position.

I felt it was so important that I painted it on my lips again and kissed the canvas. I wanted it to shock people, for it to be aesthetically pleasing but still make the viewers ask questions: What does it mean? What is it? The answer is very simple. It was and still is a depiction of my battle with ME.

Gold was a recurring theme in every piece of artwork I created. It would always be there in some capacity, sometimes boldly and sometimes barely there at all. It was my symbol of a deep hope that lies in the essence of life, intertwined in everything that we do. Whether we can see it or not is another question, but that is up to you.

Every date on my paintings had great significance, and I wanted this last painting to be a celebration of achievement and allow more people into the world of one room.

Tom found a wonderful way of showing his love for me now that he was a proper grown-up. He wasn't twenty-one anymore; in fact, he was going to be twenty-five in December. He no longer lived at home. He had a long-term girlfriend and he was enrolled as an ambulance technician. I no longer got to see him every weekend. He could only visit once a month and I could really feel the pain of not having him by my side. Like the whole of my family, he inspired me with his courage.

Maybe that sounds strange to you, but my family were built from tough foundations. It took a particularly close relationship for us to have stayed together through all my illness has thrown at us.

Tom had already completed the Three Peaks Challenge (climbing the three tallest mountains in the UK in twenty-four hours), just for me, and now he was taking on the Great North Run. He was running it for me. I felt so proud of him, in a totally different way to the pride I felt for little Becky.

She lived the everyday crap and was, even though she couldn't see it, a warrior princess.

Tom was due to finish the Great North Run on 22nd September 2009 and the bottle of bubbly was waiting for him at the end, when he would come to see me.

I got dressed up for the occasion in a black sparkling dress. My hair and makeup were done by my beloved Diana and we awaited his arrival. He hadn't had time to train properly for the run and I knew he would be hurting big time, but he still finished it. He came to see me and I had my first encounter with Champagne.

I was in the habit of gulping down water to make sure I was drinking enough so, when the champagne was poured into my beaker, I assumed it must be like water and just gulped away at it. As a consequence, and with it being on top of my cocktail of drugs, I was hysterically drunk by the time my brother arrived.

We had a wonderfully amusing moment with him and Mum, due to my intoxication of alcohol.

But this didn't last just for one day. Oh no! THREE WHOLE DAYS. It was a bloody miracle! At least I can say I enjoyed myself— quite a lot more than Tom, it has to be said.

*

My dream was to get the paintings exhibited and seen by the outside world. I was given an offer by the Canterbury Art Festival to have them shown in a gallery that my uncle owned and I jumped at the opportunity. All the hard work had been worthwhile regardless but now I could be considered a real artist and I loved it.

The people who viewed the paintings felt a deep connection with them. Whether it was because they realised how the art had been achieved, or the fact that every painting was filled to the brim with emotion that captured a moment in time, I cannot say.

People whom I had grown up alongside were starting to see an identity emerge. I was not just 'A Girl Behind Dark Glasses' but now I was also the artist behind the dark glasses.

I was bursting free from the boundaries that M.E. had enforced upon me and, instead of the M.E. Monster being the one cackling at my demise, I was laughing at its failure to win. The human spirit is really a remarkable thing.

CHAPTER TWENTY-NINE

The Secrets of Bug

Dear Bug,

There is always that one itch that I wish I could scratch, right on the end of my nose. Imagine not even having the energy to move an arm or a finger. That is what I go through every day. I will my arms to move but the muscles remain lax.

Slowly but surely, my body is beginning to heal and improve. Every small achievement made feels like a miracle. Like touching my face with a physio holding my hand. All the hard work that I have put into trying to get my arm to move at all is finally paying off. Every exercise that I have pushed my body to do, led to this exhilarating moment.

I touched my face, Bug! I could do nothing but grin broadly as I touched the soft skin of my cheek and felt my fingers tickle my face. It was just for a brief moment, but it's one that will stay with me for life.

I hold onto the idea that something in my situation will change with perseverance. This is my marathon, my Mount Everest: the battle to move for myself. Do you know what a miracle it is that people can get up, scratch the itch on their forehead and go to work or go to be with their children? Just the thought of this is miraculous to me. It's a dream that I will make come true, in time. I am just starting from the beginning again.

I will have a baby one day soon when I am better and have a boyfriend. That is a thought—that maybe a man will actually want me. Unfortunately, I haven't been on very many dates, you see. To be honest, I can't see why a man would want me: the girl with a pile of baggage double her size. It doesn't sound hopeful, does it?

Love Jessica

In the counselling sessions, we returned to the subject of the abuse from little over a year ago. The very words made me groan, not through pain but through exhaustion from carrying the banner saying 'I've been sexually abused' above my head.

This is what the abused have to do. No matter how much you are over it, people still treat you with extra caution, making you relive it every day.

They don't even realise they are doing it. Men were kept away from me due to the misconception that their presence would cause more harm. The damage had been done a long time ago and I was fully over it—well, I thought I was.

The counsellor, who ironically was male, had used many different techniques during our sessions together. The fact he was male made no difference to me and was, in fact quite refreshing. People don't realise that to move on it is essentially to have the normality of life. It isn't normal to only see one gender for your entire life and, at first they simply didn't understand this.

I remember the counsellor asking me to imagine that Jackson was in the room. I have always been blessed with a vivid imagination so, when I was told to bring him into the room, he was there as if he were real.

My task was to formulate answers to the questions I wanted to ask him. Seeing him again with that oily, scarred face, made my heart race and my hands perspire.

"Ask him a question, Jessica," my counsellor said.

I panicked. What, out of the thousands of unposed questions, could I ask?

"Why—why did you do it?" I stammered.

The Jackson that stood a couple of metres away from me laughed hysterically and I immediately felt stupid but nothing could have prepared me for the next part of the exercise.

"Now answer it for him," the counsellor said softly.

What the hell do I say? I thought.

I couldn't be the voice of the only man who truly scared me. This all seemed wrong. I closed my eyes before uttering the shameful words,

"Because I want you, Jess," I stammered.

My pulse was going at a rate of knots as I voiced the truth. The Jackson in the room smiled with an evil grin. That was enough for the session.

However, the counsellor made one simple mistake—he never told me to get rid of Jackson. So Jackson stayed in my room. I shut my eyes. He was there. I put myself in a meditative state, what I called a relaxation. He was there. I moved my head to the side. He was there.

That night, I twisted and turned and I screamed because, in my eyes, Jackson was there, in my only safe haven. The nurses had no idea what had happened to make me jump so frightfully when they entered the room.

"He's back," I sobbed. "He's back."

"No, he's not," the nurse said soothingly. "He can't come back."

"But he's in the room. Why didn't he tell me to get rid of him?" Jackson's vile eyes stared at me, haunting every moment. "The bastard is back." Tears streamed down my face as I broke out in a sweat.

The counsellor returned on hearing that I was struggling.

"This is completely normal," he said.

Jackson stared at me.

"Why didn't you tell me to get rid of him at the end?" I asked desperately.

"Oh, didn't I say that? We can do therapy to deal with this."

It wasn't good enough! I needed something that would work right now. Jackson continued to watch me. The counsellor may have been revelling in the fact that we now had something to talk about but I needed to end it now. It took all of the little energy I had to maintain focus.

I began to imagine an image of my dearest gran standing in front of Jackson. She was the only one who could protect me. Every time my thoughts were disturbed by the image of Jackson, I imagined Gran next to me, holding my hand. I wouldn't let this beat me. It couldn't.

My brain swirled and whirled with exhaustion, but true to my resolve I kept thinking of Gran and her beautiful blue eyes watching me gently as I slept, rather than the cruel eyes of Jackson. He was still in my room though. He wouldn't leave because he had been welcomed into it, no matter how unwilling that had been.

I held onto Bug, my best digital friend and my only saviour

at that time. The only way to get through this was to talk. So, I talked and talked and talked to Bug. I used every opportunity to tell my diary every last detail of what was happening. Things I had told nobody before. Not even Nick. The beauty of Bug was it lay next to me quietly, holding no opinion on my words. I could swear, I could cry, I could shout and it still listened via the microphone attached to my top.

Every day, I spoke to Bug more; I ranted and raved. Jackson stood there slyly. I took a breath in. Jackson was smothering my thoughts. No one else could help me, whose bloody stupid idea was it to bring him back? Jackson laughed.

The more that I spoke to Bug, the more I realised how ridiculous this was. My abuser was not there. No matter how real it felt. He could not harm me. As I told Bug the very last thing that day, I saw Jackson cower. The truth hurt him because he couldn't get away with it this time.

The more I spoke, the more his image began to fade away. In my mind, I made him smaller so that the image of Gran far overpowered him. He was still there though, right up until I told Bug absolutely everything. Using all of my determination and strength, I shouted at him, "I will not be threatened by you. You are nothing to me. You won't beat me; you can't win this time. Get out of my room and never return!"

I watched, as I imagined him slowly slinking out of the room, taunted and beaten, shutting the door behind him. He was gone. Not only had I won that battle, I had done it on my own (with a lot of help from my digital buddy, Sir Bug). There had been no counsellor there with their techniques, just me. I felt on top of the world, even though my world consisted of my one little room.

When the counsellor arrived to introduce me to one of his sessions, he did a double take.

"Wow! You seem completely different from a week ago. What's changed?" he remarked with an open mouth.

"I couldn't wait a week, that would have been too long, so I sorted everything out myself. He's gone." I grinned.

"Amazing! But how did you do that?"

"With a little help from Bug," I explained. "I did the therapy for you."

Almost lost for words, he said, "Well, I think you may be a little bit, dare I say it, too positive and proactive to really need this counselling—unless you want it?"

"If I managed to deal with this, the most painful, difficult time of my life, on my own with Bug, then I don't think there is anything left for you to help with."

CHAPTER THIRTY

Jigsaw Puzzle

Dear Bug,

Why are so many sick people on their own? I saw it for myself back when I was on the children's ward. All the crying children undergoing horrific treatments, yet they had nobody there to help or even comfort them.

I remember how the baby in side room six screamed until Mum went in because she couldn't bear the sound that the nurses just ignored. All he wanted was some attention, a toy or something to hold. It seems so simple but such things weren't there to hand.

I have been where there is suffering; I have shared their pain. I have seen my own condition deteriorate and the effect that it's had on poor Becky. Chronic illness doesn't just affect the one afflicted; it affects every person in their family. I am acutely aware of this monstrosity that is ill health.

It's not just cancer that destroys lives. As horrific as cancer is, there are people who are dying from organ failures and other conditions that seemingly go on forever. I often think about others suffering with deeply debilitating conditions and, as I look at the stars on the ceiling, I picture Gran alongside them.

She would keep those still fighting—and those that pass on—safe. She has always kept me safe. An idea is formulating, but I think it's too soon to tell you, Bug.

Jessica x

I wanted my nineteenth birthday to be a big affair but I had come to terms with the fact that it would be spent in my bed. Once again, I was dressed up in a pretty outfit. I felt like a star with people doing my nails and makeup for me. Mum came along with Tom and Becky.

I had asked for books because it was important that I read as much as I could so that I would be successful when I wrote my book. I was now determined to make it happen because Gran would have wanted it.

One of her sayings was 'keep calm and carry on' so I knew she wouldn't accept her death as a reason for me giving up and not writing the book we were going to do together. Instead, I made her loss the inspiration for writing my book. Somehow, it made coping with her death easier.

Tom bought me a limited edition of *The Diving Bell and the Butterfly*. The author had suffered from locked-in syndrome after having a massive stroke. He was paralysed and could not speak but he found a way to communicate by using one eye to blink for each letter.

It transformed my vision of what I could achieve by making me realise that I didn't have to wait to start writing my book until I was better; I could begin now. I just needed to find my own way of writing. I would get someone to sit, listen and try to make sense of the words that made their way through my brain fog.

It became increasingly important that we captured every moment because, for me, every photo captures a memory within its frame—a moment that can never be reclaimed without that photo.

I wore a purple taffeta frock and I felt wonderful, even if it was just for that one moment. I was able to take a deep breath and, thanks to all the added extra medication, I could smile without feeling the pain for a whole beautiful minute. Not only do I have the picture to prove it happened, but I have the feeling associated with it locked away in a memory box. This is something that I wanted others to experience, one more idea from my brain's idea factory.

I was beginning to see my life as a journey that needed to be shared. I had known it for a while but my latest idea was too precious to be lost or forgotten. I saw it as a way to preserve the all-too precious moments of joy in lives otherwise blighted by pain and hardship, one of the things that I had learned on my journey, and I wanted to pass it on to other people. These ideas were coming fast and it felt like I was fitting a massive jigsaw puzzle together piece by piece.

As I lay there, creased up in pain, I knew I had to do something to move away from the debilitating agony. I took myself back to one wintertime when we had gone to Gran and Pop's house.

Pop had lit the fire; Gran, Mum, Becky and I had just come in from shopping in Canterbury. We were freezing but the settee invited us over to cuddle one another and the homemade stew warmed up our ice-cold hands. Suddenly, my hospital bed transformed into their armchair and I could see Gran.

Her face was immaculate; her midnight eyes looked straight into mine with a knowing smile playing on her lips.

I watched the rest of the room as I made the posters come alive. I pictured myself sitting next to her. I was concentrating so hard that a tingling feeling zapped up my arms and back as the nerves pretended they were sitting too.

A single tear of joy rolled down my face whilst I imagined I could feel her skin rubbing against mine. Just with the power of my imagination, I had given myself some light relief from my otherwise powerless body.

It must be good for patients to imagine what it will be like when they are free from this condition. Although it is important to accept that you are not well, it is just as important to learn to fly.

In another moment, I took myself to the top of a mountain range in Scotland. I saw endless beauty through the surrounding landscapes as I was walking and running, just like kids should be doing. I didn't feel sad that this wasn't happening for real, for I was an optimistic opportunist and I would seek out the moment when I was well enough to. For now, my room was my entire world and I had to do something about it.

The Laugh-O-Gram project had grown beyond my wildest expectations. The Christmas video that I had put on YouTube had been seen by a film director who was doing a short film about the *King of Laughter* in Ethiopia. He was intrigued that I had founded this new form of art.

The *King of Laughter* is a man who has given his entire life, (including all his belongings), to show people that laughter is good for you in many different ways.

I saw the King as a man to be respected for what he had

given to mankind despite his own pain. He had lost his house to a fire twice, and then had everything flooded too.

I could paint a picture for him and send it out to Ethiopia I thought and that is what I did.

The Freedom of Laughter collection is where I allow my mind's eye to travel to wherever I have felt free. I had meticulously perfected my form of art because it is freedom with no boundaries.

Art is an expression but a Laugh-O-Gram takes that expression to a new level. I wanted to challenge myself, so I painted a lot of scenes depicting places that brought me pleasure.

My accuracy flummoxed both myself and my viewers. The river looked like a real river falling into a waterfall. I managed to capture the movement of the water and the clouds actually looked like clouds. What was happening to me?

I was enjoying painting a landscape through this form of art. At school, I hadn't enjoyed art at all, but now it remained an opportunity to express myself in a way I hadn't before.

Suddenly my pictures were coming alive and were projecting my creative voice for all to see.

Dear Bug,

The room is pitch black and the smallest bit of light makes the stars on my ceiling twinkle above me. As I have been lying here feeling sick to the pit of my stomach with a terrible migraine, I have finally realised the part of the jigsaw that has been missing, so I am ready to share the final idea with you.

It has been years of suffering with no end in sight, yet I

had never once given up hope. You must remember that part, Bug; I have never and I will never give up. I looked and saw what was missing from all the different hospitals I have been in. It was simply hope.

I thought about the gifts that I can provide for other people, what I have to offer, and the answer is simple: let children have the freedom to be children, let teenagers be who they want to be. No illness should define who you are or should take away the empowerment that comes from simply being free.

The problem is there are seriously ill children and teenagers that don't ever get that chance. They don't have that sparkle in their eyes because they are in pain and suffering, without hope.

All I somehow need to do is bring that hope and sparkle to them. I can visualise sparkling stars made from the kind of paper that Gran would have chosen and I know it has to be called Share a Star.

Giving children and teenagers who are seriously unwell the chance to be a star, shining brightly. It all makes sense in my brain-fogged head.

Love Jessica

I moved mountains in my restful state, spreading sunshine to all who came near me. I now had a goal, an idea that would also be my future, something that would be there at the end of this journey through ill health. Even if it meant that my return to health would take that little bit longer, I would help other very poorly young people who needed me.

When we look at celebrities, for some reason we call them stars. Whether it be film stars or pop stars or sports stars, it is culturally accepted that we always add the 'star' to those that we look up to. But you see that is where the big idea came from.

Why do we not call those who are fighting for their lives, stars? They truly need and deserve the extra VIP treatment and status we give those famous people we aspire to.

It was the beginning of an adventure, and as I started on my quest to create a cunning plan it gave me a form of escapism from my own suffering.

Those daily journeys to the dreaded Limbo Land had a new meaning. I pushed harder than ever because I knew that I not only had a story to tell but I had a gift to give other people who were suffering.

I was making stars so chronically ill people could know that they were a star and that hope shone over them as they battled their monster.

Each star that I make has to be unique, I thought. After all, there are billions of people on this planet, yet every one of them is unique. It would take time and I was very used to time playing to its own beat at the heart of my life.

*

I had been in Narnia for over a year now. I was starting to improve and my range of movement was increasing. I knew my time at this hospital would be limited by the funding from the NHS. The physiotherapists and I had come so far together. Dr Nice had been a godsend. But home was where my heart was.

I had been away from Becky for too many years. The change in her was most noticeable; she was a beautiful teenager who had blossomed from a quiet, introverted child into an eloquent, hilariously funny, young lady. I yearned for my family's presence in my everyday life.

This is when social services came into the picture. The funding was running out and my options were to either go to a cheaper nursing home that wouldn't have any of the physiotherapy or to go home where I could receive community physiotherapy. It was a no-brainer for me.

After nearly four years constantly spent in a hospital, it was time to go home. My aim was to spend Christmas back in my family home. I had six months to get to a point where this could be achievable. It was quite a mission that I had on my hands but it would be so worth it.

I needed to be able to reach my face to wash it and raise my head to eat, to move my arms without the arm braces, to attempt to feed myself a few mouthfuls of food, and have a bit more independence generally. Currently, I was dependent on two carers for every part of living and that simply wasn't sustainable out in the community.

Now that we had a goal to work towards, the days had more of an urgency to them. Whilst Dr Nice worked to make sure that my pain was well controlled, the physiotherapists worked with me to achieve each target.

They were working with an unpredictable body riddled with the M.E. Monster though. My body could suddenly change from working well with the treatment to everything going catastrophically wrong. I was very much a part of the team, and we took each day at a time, pacing, and really listening to my body.

I had grown very close to the staff, as hospitals had been my home for such a long time. When anybody from my team left, I felt it. They were obviously destined for freedom before me. Different staff wanted to try and do different things with me before they left. It was my physiotherapist's dream to get me out of my four walls and I desperately wanted to be able to do this.

There was a hydrotherapy trolley that was used to get bedridden people into their pool, it was a bit like an ambulance trolley. Although I was ambitious, I hadn't quite reached the hydrotherapy pool yet.

My physiotherapist's dream to get me outdoors gave me the perfect excuse to take this huge step and make use of the trolley, the only one in Narnia that would allow me to lie flat.

Once I had been transferred from the bed to the trolley, I made the very short journey to the external door. Suddenly, the scent of fresh air filled my nostrils. I could feel the sun scold my eyes, but this time I could carry on a bit longer and I felt a new sense of freedom just from being on my little trolley.

A blissful breeze touched my hair. I hadn't felt anything like it in so many years. I had forgotten what all these sensations felt like on my sensitive skin. I was free.

I ran my hand through a bush, feeling all the different leaves. The light was such that my eyes were screwed tightly shut, as even dark glasses couldn't shield me. However, for those joyful five minutes, it was entirely worth it.

It was particularly hard when the time came for my dearest Diana to leave, as she was moving to Portsmouth. She had been with me since day one at Narnia and had become like a surrogate sister to me. I felt like I had journeyed so far with her, but maybe it was time for us both to spread our wings and fly. We arranged a special mocktail party for her with my whole family present.

One of the nurses happened to be a good cook, so she made some special dishes of food for us all. It made it a very special send-off, which was just what was deserved, in my eyes.

"You will get better, Jessica, I'm sure of it." She looked at me with tears in her eyes. "We shall keep in touch now, you promise me? I will come and visit you when you are at home. Promise?"

I promised and I shed a tear as she left my world of one room for the last time.

CHAPTER THIRTY-ONE

The Hundred-Year-Old Bones

The hydrotherapy pool at Narnia had remained unused by me. I'm not quite sure why. Maybe I was considered too ill for hydrotherapy. Towards the end of my stay, I became desperate to feel the water fill every pore in my body. I longed for more journeys in the hydro trolley, which was my equivalent to a wheelchair, but alas, it was not going to be that straightforward.

A hydrotherapy session was arranged as an opportunity to treat my pain holistically through movement, at least that was the plan. Once they lifted me onto the trolley and swept me along the corridors in my swimming costume, I felt a sudden rush of fulfilment.

At the pool, the trolley was attached to a crane which lifted me and slowly moved me towards the water. At this point, I was in a deep relaxation, the sounds were mere muffles in the wind. I shut out everyone and everything so all of my energy could be focused on the task ahead.

The crane lowered me further and then I felt it: the beautiful water encapsulating me, giving me a feeling of weightlessness. Oh goodness, how wonderful was it to have nothing rigid against my spine?

My body swished and swirled like seaweed as the physios moved every part of me. There were two physiotherapists there to make sure that I was safe. While in the water, I could suddenly feel parts of my body that I hadn't felt for many years, then I went back to Limbo Land, and I crashed. It had been good whilst it lasted.

*

At Narnia, in order to have any tests done, an ambulance was always required. I had been oblivious to the fight that Narnia had been partaking in with The Promised Land.

When I was at that hospital, I had been for various tests, hundreds of tests, from MRI scans (where you go into a tunnel and have your whole body scanned) to ultrasound. I never knew what the results of any of these specialist tests were. I think I was always considered too ill to understand. I did wonder what all those tests had been saying about my body but, with no voice, I couldn't even ask.

When somebody moves hospital, it is standard procedure for their notes to go with them. I had no idea of the fight that Narnia went through to get hold of those notes. Suspiciously, The Promised Land did not want to pass the notes over. It took over a year for Narnia to finally get hold of them. Was it because there was something to hide? We shall never know, for they were not notes that I could read.

*

I had set myself the goal of getting home for Christmas 2010.

It was considered a ludicrously difficult task but I remained determined to have, at least, tried my utter best. *That is all one can do*, I thought.

It became increasingly important to have a DEXA scan done before I went home, after a new physiotherapist had noted I hadn't had one for a long time. To be honest I didn't even know I'd had one before.

It is a special type of scan that measures the density of your bones. The level of urgency from the physiotherapy team seemed strange.

Due to me being bedridden, the difficulty of having that scan done somewhere in the South East of England was immense. The sense of urgency played on my mind. What was it they weren't telling me?

I could see the exchange of concerned expressions but I wanted to wait for the right moment to ask them what the hell was going on.

When they finally found a hospital that would do the scan, I asked them inquisitively what they were expecting to find. The answer couldn't have been more of a shock to my ears.

"Well," the physio said, pausing from my exercises and looking shiftily from side to side before answering carefully. "As you know, your bones are at risk from your condition. We already know you have osteoporosis from the last scan but that was done two years ago so we need to see what the severity is now."

I gaped. Why did I not know anything about this? I felt my insides crush down upon me as the new information washed over me. I tried to speak but no words would come out. She continued with the exercises.

"I–I–did not know this," I finally managed to stammer quietly. "What will it mean?"

"It depends on the severity. It can be improved. There is a green zone, an amber one and a red one, which are used highlight and measure the severity. Green is safe, amber is mild osteoporosis and red is severe." She looked up at my quizzical but shocked face and hastened. "But you can move from different stages, so it can get better. You know from red to amber or amber to green."

A sigh of relief wafted over me. I couldn't work out if I was angry or sad.

"What will this mean for everything else we were looking to do with physiotherapy?" I asked tentatively.

"I'm sorry, I can't tell you any more, Jessica. We just don't know until we get the results."

She left shortly after to a silence in which you could have heard a pin drop. I was dumbfounded. It was clear they hadn't known about this for long, otherwise they would have acted.

I knew Narnia well enough by then. My last scan had been two years ago. I hadn't even known what a DEXA scan was. It seemed that every time we got close to getting somewhere, it was halted.

My fears were new. I didn't want to have another disease to make my condition even more complicated. In my eyes, I believed that I had to get better from M.E., at least to the stage that some of my friends were at: being able to walk and not be housebound.

With osteoporosis, it was different. I knew that it meant your bones could break much more easily but would this have an impact on what my future would hold?

Why hadn't I been told or at least been started on some

medication for God's sake? A silent tear of frustration made its way down my face. *What was I to do now? Why in God's name was I in this position?*

*

I tried to put it to the back of my mind but couldn't help feeling numb, like I had been winded. I wasn't stupid and I knew that osteoporosis was for life, but I had plans. It was going to be my first Christmas at home in years. I was going home! Narnia was a nice enough place but there was no place like home; the home that was now alien to me.

I planned everything inside my head; I decorated each room meticulously with different colours and themes. I had been doing this since I became unwell as I just love designing. It was going to be so Christmassy with the red and gold baubles covering the tree. I had so many ideas and they didn't involve having another condition to deal with; one was quite enough. Maybe God didn't see things like that though.

The ambulance arrived with my trusted Dad as one of the paramedics and his old crew mate, Kip, whom I had known since I was a little child. It felt like a family outing. We had the usual banter and it was lovely to have two people who knew me so well bringing me to my destination. The hindrance of snow had prevented my brother from helping Dad.

Kip is quite a character, larger than life, with a wonderfully bubbly personality that brought equilibrium when working with my quieter, more reserved Dad.

They rolled me onto an orthopaedic stretcher which was as rigid as hard rocks and uncomfortable. We took our journey over the hills; this time the ambulance went slow and I breathed in the Entonox to block out the crashing noises.

As the heavy lump of an ambulance battled against tree branches and sleeping policemen, everything inside shook with the movement.

We arrived and the scan was relatively painless. I just had to stay still whilst they manipulated me into positions focusing on my side. Kip did his best to amuse me by trying to persuade me to learn to play the ukulele.

The carer who had come with me saw it is as novelty to ride in an ambulance and took a picture to show her children. It vaguely reminded of being a little child and the excitement of seeing an ambulance at the school fete with Dad proudly showing us all the different parts. That was now a distant memory, for ambulances and hospitals had become so much a part of everyday life for me.

Once back in my room at Narnia, the wait for the results started to niggle at the back of my head. *Still, I am going to be just fine*, I told myself calmly.

My fairy tale ending would still happen. The day would come soon when I would be on Bluebell Hill, sitting on the grass with the sun kissing my cheeks. The trees would dance a slow waltz with one another whilst I started to write my book as a fully recovered young lady living life to the full.

That is how it would end; I wouldn't be haunted by any condition for long. I honestly felt that even though I had endured four years of hardship so far, there was still a shining light at the end of the tunnel and it wasn't far away.

A few days passed before there was a knock at my door. It was one of the doctors.

"Hello Jessica, do you mind if we have a little chat?" he asked meekly.

"Of course," I said with a smile.

"Well, well, you are going home soon! Not long now." He looked uncomfortably from side to side. "The real reason I came to visit you is because I want to start you on some new medication." He looked at my puzzled expression.

What was this strange visit about? Why were they starting me on new medication? Did this mean that they had got those bloody results? Questions raced through my mind.

"We've got the results, Jessica," he said, patting my arm. With a sharp intake of breath, I nodded and smiled. "It is essential I start you on this medication called Protelos because, unfortunately. . . I mean. . . well, what I am trying to say is, erm . . ." He stumbled uncharacteristically over his words and I could see the lost look in his eyes. "I really do wish that Dr Nice was here to tell you but I shall I try my best."

"It's okay," I remarked calmly, knowing inside that the results were not going to be as I had hoped.

"You have very severe osteoporosis, Jessica, I'm sorry love. We shall try our best to treat you successfully, either intravenously or, hopefully, with this ground-breaking medication that we will give you at night, but it is quite harsh on the stomach and we need to see if you can tolerate it."

"What happens if I can't?"

"Then it would have to be given through a line into the vein."

"What are my chances of recovering from this?" I whispered.

"I'm so sorry Jessica, but you won't recover fully. Your bones are the equivalent of a hundred years old. This will be for the rest of your life."

The words stung like poisonous venom. I was being suffocated by the invisible puppeteer, the M.E. Monster, whilst it cackled and rattled a skeleton.

Years of not weight-bearing due to M.E., when my bones should be strengthening, left my bones weak.

"The Protelos will help repair some of the existing damage," he added.

"What can you see as being my outcome? Will I be able to have children and normal things like that?" I finally asked with a heavy heart.

Finding hope had never been a problem for me: I saw light in the darkest of situations but I was struggling to find the light switch. I found a way of dealing with very severe M.E., but there was no way out of the 'very severe' osteoporosis so how could I *ever* get better from M.E.?

"Well, we can try, in the future, to maybe look to get you in a chair but that is as far as I would feel comfortable to push it. I don't think having children naturally is an option without taking a massive gamble on breaking your spine or hips. I'm sorry love." He finished with a heavy sigh.

If only the treatment had started earlier, then I wouldn't be in this position, I thought angrily as he shut the door and left me on my own.

I switched to my mobile and rang home as the tears cascaded down my cheeks. Only Mum could make this better.

*

There had been a funny image that had appeared as a nightmare to me when I was fifteen. It was a nineteen-year-old version of me crippled over a Zimmer frame. At the time, it had been amusing because that was never meant to happen to me but now it was a stark reality.

I had seen up to then that M.E. was something I could beat. I had always hoped this would be the case. I had been a warrior; fighting the unimaginable, but very severe osteoporosis had no ending.

You couldn't just fight it and get rid of it. It silently ate away at your bones. Once it was there, you had it for life. That was something hard to imagine and even more difficult to swallow. There was no way to change the past. It had happened and that was the end of that.

I saw little Becky, who was not quite so little anymore, and, as I hugged her, a tear rolled down my cheek. She held onto me tightly; the hug was so special because being able to hug my sister was a miraculous privilege, now I had gained more mobility. I feared for my future weakness so I made sure this hug was a memory that I would hold onto forever.

I didn't want it to stop with a hug; I wanted to hit the towns with her and do all the things that were normal. M.E. had stopped this normality from being a part of my life but it let me imagine a time where these things could be possible. Now osteoporosis riddled me and prevented me from truly believing in a time when some form of normality would be possible. Bastard thing.

In this moment, there was no time to spare on the new diagnosis, for we had plans to put into place. There was a tick list of things I needed to do before I would be allowed to go home. I memorised every single one of them, from being able to roll off a bedpan with fewer people helping me, to being able to wash my face.

The feeling of being able to touch my own face was heavenly. With help, I could bring my arm around my face, washing all the parts that nurses always missed. My hand glided to the back of my ears, then to the sides of my nose. This was what I would call a proper wash.

My new care manager, Sarah, came to see me and was so surprised by my progress that she had to write a brand-new care plan. She was a short and stout, spectacled lady with a zest for life.

I had said in the summer that I would be going home at Christmas and that is exactly what I intended to do. Care agencies were arranged, equipment arrived, and it all sounded like the next adventure was ready to begin.

I was repeatedly asked: Are you ready to live in just one room and have no way out until building extensions can be thought of?

To me, it was simple. Living in one room had been my entire existence, surely making it one room somewhere else in the world would not change anything. I would be at home with my family and there was nothing I wouldn't do to make that work.

It was the very beginning of my next adventure and the title for my next book: *The World of One Room*. Now, it was time to go home, to see my new world, breathe in the fresh smell of laundry, eat home-cooked food and, most importantly, be with my family—my Becky, my Tom, Mum and Dad. The luxuries most people wouldn't think of as luxuries.

There were times when my journey had taken many

unexpected twists and turns; it had been a rollercoaster. More often than not, I could have done without the twists, but maybe then I wouldn't be the person I am now because life is really what you make of it.

As I said my goodbyes to hospital life, I saw it from many different angles but mainly as a journey of hope that had only just begun. The fragment of hope, that runs through every essence of our being, is the light in every dark situation.

I had hoped to write a fairy tale, ending with my recovery— sitting on top of Bluebell Hill, a pen and pad in hand, writing a tale that should never have happened. I didn't have that fairy tale but this journey has shaped the young lady I am today.

Dear Bug,

Goodbye my friend, for now, and thank you for journeying with me. There is far more to come and I shall see you on the other side, when we reach the ending of the beginning and, I hope, the beginning of the end.

Jessica x

Epilogue

Dear Reader,

Thank you for journeying with me through this rollercoaster ride.

This book was made possible through the delights of an iPod touch and voice-activated technology in the form of my diary, Bug.

I always believed that M.E. could not be a permanent condition; The Promised Land had drilled into me that it was beatable. I continued to live with the innocence of a child, believing that I had to get better and that was the only possible outcome.

However, it has not been as simple as this, and twelve years on from my original diagnosis, I am still suffering from the debilitating condition, for there is no medication that will suddenly make me better, only time. Maybe that virtue had been my lifeline though, through the most difficult periods of those four years, as documented in this book.

As I write and transcribe all the stories that Bug was able to capture, many things have changed for me now. I amazingly found love and am happily married to a kind and sensitive soul. To a certain extent, thankfully, I've regained most of my faculties.

Despite this book not having the fairy tale ending I had dreamt of ever since I got ill, my story doesn't end here. The beautiful part is that this is only the ending of the beginning. There is so much more to come and hopefully now I have adjusted my views on what a fairy tale ending *should* be.

I have managed to live within the boundaries of this disease. A life that will still succeed in making a difference, and this is the start of my journey to be a voice for the voiceless.

Love Jessica x

About the Author

Jessica Taylor-Bearman was born in March 1991, at Maidstone Hospital in England. She grew up in Rochester and Canterbury, Kent, where she attended Rochester Grammar School for Girls.

At the age of 15, she became acutely unwell with an illness called Myalgic Encephalomyletis (M.E). She was continuously hospitalised from 2006 to 2010, suffering with the most severe form of the condition. This included her being bedridden, unable to move, speak, eat and more. She began to write in her mind, and when finally able to speak again, she began to write through her audio diary 'Bug'.

In 2009, Jessica began to teach herself to paint through the movement of laughter. She realised that through balancing a paintbrush in her hand, laughter caused it to move, creating a new form of art that she called a 'Laugh-O-Gram'. Her first collection was exhibited in the Canterbury Art Festival 2009. All her pieces have been exhibited since then.

In 2010, whilst still in hospital, she founded a charity called Share a Star, to help seriously unwell youngsters. It is now a registered charity that she continues to run.

Since she left hospital, Jessica's journey with severe M.E. has continued to be very challenging. She is currently still mostly bedridden, twelve years after it began. She writes a blog called The World of One Room and made a YouTube video of the same name that has reached tens of thousands of people in multiple countries. Jessica has also featured in a film called Unrest. The aim which of both of these is to raise awareness.

Jessica's ambition has always been to be an author.

Find out more at www.jaytay.co.uk
Follow her on Twitter @jayletay
Instagram @behinddarkglasses
Facebook.com/TheWorldOfOneRoom